Hello!

Hello!
And Every Little Thing That Matters

Kate Edwards

palgrave
macmillan

First published 2016 by
PALGRAVE MACMILLAN

The author has asserted their right to be identified as the author of this work in accordance with the Copyright, Designs and Patents Act 1988.

Palgrave Macmillan in the UK is an imprint of Macmillan Publishers Limited, registered in England, company number 785998, of Houndmills, Basingstoke, Hampshire, RG21 6XS.

Palgrave Macmillan in the US is a division of Nature America, Inc., One New York Plaza, Suite 4500, New York, NY 10004-1562.

Palgrave Macmillan is the global academic imprint of the above companies and has companies and representatives throughout the world.

Hardback ISBN: 978–1–137–48970–8
E-PUB ISBN: 978–1–137–48972–2
E-PDF ISBN: 978–1–137–48971–5
DOI: 10.1057/9781137489715

Distribution in the UK, Europe and the rest of the world is by Palgrave Macmillan®, a division of Macmillan Publishers Limited, registered in England, company number 785998, of Houndmills, Basingstoke, Hampshire RG21 6XS.

Library of Congress Cataloging-in-Publication Data

Edwards, Kate, 1967–
    Hello! : and every little thing that matters / Kate Edwards.
      pages cm
    Includes index.
    ISBN 978–1–137–48970–8 (alk. paper)
      1. Customer relations. I. Title.

HF5415.5.E27 2015
658.8′12—dc23   2015022375

A catalogue record for the book is available from the British Library.

Printed in the United States of America.

Contents

Acknowledgments

I am incredibly pleased to have worked with my agent, Lynn Johnston, and my editor, Laurie Harting. They are a dynamic duo in the literary world, and I am so appreciative to have had the chance to collaborate with them both. Many thanks to the team at Palgrave Macmillan for making what was a daunting prospect into a challenging, interesting, and fun experience.

This wouldn't have been possible without having had numerous incredible opportunities throughout my career. The two most notable are Balthazar and Per Se and I am grateful to both Keith McNally and Thomas Keller and their stellar teams for granting me the opportunity to learn and grow while employed in their restaurants.

Sincere thanks to my clients, colleagues, friends, and collaborators; you helped to bring this book to life. Your stories and generosity are much appreciated and *"Hello!"* bears your imprint. Many thanks to Yvonne and Marco Ackermann, Harmony Trujilo, Jean Francois Pilon, Michael Todd Belasco, Jeffrey Dyksterhouse, Nora McAniff, Paul Bouchard, Marco Maccioni, Sirio Maccioni, Jessica Wilson, Adam Weiner, Veronica Jenkins, York Ast, Judy Rosemarin, Michael Gibney, Igor Apraiz, Jeff David, Michel Darmon, Carlos Suarez, Cindi Byun, Nancy Cohen, Mark Schoifet, Andrew Sole, Stephen Covello, Andre Fries, Michael Conlon, Steve Zagor, Phoebe Damrosch, Alison Cayne, Joe Johnson, and Mary Cleaver.

Special acknowledgment goes to my husband Reinhold Heller; my friends Carolyn Paddock, Susan Pasquantonio, Jennifer Sagawa, and Michou Szabo; to my parents Charles and Mary Edwards; and to my brother and sister-in-law Michael Edwards and Danielle Morris. Thank you all for your unflagging belief in me; I could not have done this without you.

Thank you for reading, enjoy.

Introduction

I conduct an exercise with my students when I teach a class called "An Introduction to Service." In the class I pose the question "What is service?" and ask the class for answers. The answers are almost always the same; the students throw out words and concepts, such as "hospitality, caring, nurturing, listening, serving, creating an experience, the flow, the timing, everything feels right, they can relax, they feel good." These are all correct; we want our guests to feel all of those things. The next part of the question is "why is service important?" and this is where folks get stymied. It is natural that people think of service in terms of hospitality and caring, but they often forget that service is about sales. I always say, "service is the engine of sales"; without service there is no money to be made.

That's right, service and sales are conjoined concepts designed to make a business successful and profitable. When your service is good, people are more likely to patronize your business than when the service is shaky, insincere, or inconsistent. When I ask people if they would rather patronize a restaurant where the food was outstanding but the service was okay or a restaurant where the service was outstanding and the food was okay, most people say they would go where the service is great. I always use the example of the Starbucks where they know your name or of the diner where they remember your order. The coffee or food is good, consistent, and tasty but certainly not unique or stellar. Indeed, the service is what brings us back and what stays in our memories.

Because service is about an "experience," we have to take all parts of the guest experience into account. The environment, how it is designed and maintained, the timing, and the consistency of the operation are all facets of the guest experience that come under the umbrella of service. In this book I will share that the way people experience your business tacitly can have a huge impact on their interest in spending money and I'll shine a light on the way in which people are hardwired to become a regular of your business. I'll share insights such as my principle of "I notice = I care" that can help transform your team from generally good into generally great service ambassadors. I will address language and the nuances of verbal, vocal, and nonverbal communication that sends powerful messages to your guests. And I will share the importance of one little word: Hello.

Service is a conversation; it is not a monologue or a lecture. Service has an impact on your guests that will make a difference to your bottom line. Service is also an inspiring and noble endeavor. Those of us in any service-oriented business can all share stories of making a difference in someone's day, of helping a stranger, of solving a problem, of creating a wonderful solution, and of making a difference in someone's life. Service about making an impact on another human being and it is about making their life better. This is service, and it is incredibly rewarding.

I wrote *"Hello!"* as a handbook for owners, managers, and their teams that can act as a reference book. It answers the bigger question of what service is and why service is important and also offers tips and tricks for making a positive impression on your guests and staff. Your staff is part of the service equation because staff members deliver service firsthand to your customers. So we must always be mindful and supportive of our teams and enable them to help our guests as frequently and easily as possible. My goal is that *"Hello!"* helps you deliver service that makes a difference and that makes your business thrive.

CHAPTER 1

Hello: The First Important Thing

Surprise and Awe

One evening I walked into my neighborhood Staples. It was about 5:00 p.m. so it was not yet rush hour. I followed two women through the door, and as we entered, I heard the cashier say "Hello!" to the women ahead of me. They were taken by surprise and looked warily at one another. As we progressed into the store and past the line of cashiers, we heard a chorus of "Good evening," "Welcome to Staples," and "Hello" from every cashier on duty. The women ahead of me were clearly confused and almost unsettled. They were in Staples, not exactly a bastion of warm and welcoming service. Or was it? As we turned the corner, a manager greeted me with "Good evening, ma'am, may I help you find something?" I declined and went up the stairs. At the top of the stairs was another employee and again another cheery "Hello!" was offered.

While the women in front of me were clearly put off by this effusion, I have to say that part of the confusion was that none of us expected this friendliness in Staples. It was enthusiastic, warm, helpful customer service, not the usual experience when buying office supplies. When I went to the checkout counter, the response was equally enthusiastic, and my experience ended with the last cashier nearest the door calling out as I left, "Have a great night!" I thought to myself, "Was this a fluke?" but the next time I went into the store, my experience was the same and even in different Staples stores, the attention to customers was the same.

So what did the store employees provide for me? Was it free stuff? No. Was it more variety? No. Was it a fantasyland of office supplies? No! It was acknowledgment. You are the customer. You are in our store. You might have questions. I am here for you. And how did they let me know that? By graciously saying "Hello!" Wow, that was easy.

The first and most important thing you can say to your customers is hello. Hello starts conversations; it indicates that you are curious, interested, and friendly and open. If there is one sentiment you must arm your staff with to have an incredible impact on your customers, it is some version of hello.

How you say hello is important. This is the first point of contact with your guests, and the word is an easy and gracious gesture that is often overlooked. Hello carries social power that greases the wheels of human rapport; yet too often this and other aspects of hospitality are lost, along with the opportunity to set the proper stage for the rest of the customers' experience. One of the first things you must do is train your staff on the greeting. While you may not have to teach your staff the word "hello" (they know it and use it every day), it is essential to take this common greeting a step further by crafting the tone and substance of the greeting to reflect your business personality and uphold your core values. This way you ensure that the core message of your business will be lived out every time a staff member greets a customer on the phone or in person.

The greeting is the first of many important "moments of service" that make up the customer experience. It is your first opportunity to connect first-time customers with your staff and your brand, and it is the best opportunity to foster a consistent relationship between your repeat guests and your company. The greeting can happen a number of times, both remotely (on the phone or online) or in person. At many businesses the moment when a greeting may occur can vary; you may have many moments when your customer is greeted. As in my experience in Staples, the greeting can happen with each new person a customer interacts with; that is, the greeting happens not just once but many times.

In a large office building, the first person someone meets might be at the reception desk or even at the security desk. At a restaurant, the first person customers meet is at the host stand, and at a hotel, that person is at the front door. At a medical office, that first encounter happens at the reception desk. These points represent an opportunity to make a good and powerful first impression; this first greeting is essential because it sets the tone for the experience. Going to security for an ID badge should not make your clients feel like they have just gone to visit someone in jail. There should be no intrusive questioning ("What's your name? Who are you meeting? What time is your meeting? What floor?") nor should there be a difference between the reception your clients get on one floor and the one they get on another. This initial moment must reflect the ethos of your business and start the relationship off on the right foot, a relationship that will continue with each step your customer takes into your business.

The second greeting could happen when customers arrive on the desired floor, when they are escorted to an examining room or arrive at a specific office. This next contact person should make an effort to greet customers and help them feel welcome and valued. This second greeting is a virtual second base for your client: it could result in a home run or in a total loss. This moment of service is essential to your success, and you need to make sure you have a trained professional there to handle this important task. At this point, your client has made it through the front door, has traversed some hallways or yards, and has now arrived safely at his or her destination. The second greeting will enhance or dissipate the mood set up from the prior greeting, and whether your customer knows it or not, he or she is waiting to see if you succeed or fail. Customers who were treated abruptly or coldly at the first greeting point (the front desk agent gets their attention by yelling "Next!" rather than by saying something like "Welcome to the Hyatt!"), then the second greeting becomes all the more important and tells guests whether they can relax and enjoy the experience or should avoid the staff for the rest of their time there. For example, in a hotel when that bellman comes to help arriving guests and with a smile says "Welcome to the Hyatt, let me show you to your room," those guests can now relax and enjoy being the passenger, so to speak, in the service experience.

Moreover, there is a public aspect to the greeting. The first greeting is often uttered in front of other people and thus sets waiting customers up for what will happen when it is their turn. In other words, even if you have a guest who is a control freak and is not very comfortable in the passenger seat (doesn't care for pleasantries, wants to move on without a big fuss, doesn't want to hear the spiel, but just wants what he wants when he wants it), your staff members must still be consistent in their greeting because it can be overheard by others and lets them know what they can expect from your business.

When I was consulting at The Palm Court, the famous restaurant at The Plaza Hotel, arguably one of the best-known hotels in New York City, I often helped out at the host stand with greeting and checking in guests while the managers hustled to make service flow without interruption. On one rainy day the tables were turning very slowly, as many parties had arrived late for their reservations due to the rain and the traffic. With each new arrival, more and more hungry people were waiting to be seated. There was no separate waiting room, and the foyer became filled with people. I greeted every guest warmly on arrival and then honestly told each person the wait time. I also took great pains to take a moment to chat with the waiting guests. Many were very kind and understood the situation. Some were not so nice, but I kept my cool, exuded warmth and calm, and continued greeting and seating the waiting throng.

Here's the thing: people notice when you are friendly, warm, and consistent during stressful times, and on that day more than one person complimented me on my demeanor and consistency in interacting with each arriving guest. There was no hiding the fact that we were behind; I was very clear with each guest, and then I remembered each specifically and took time to give each party updates. But it was the greeting that was consistent, and people overheard that. That consistency gave them faith that they would get a table and that it would be worth the wait. If I had gotten stressed out and had started calling out names rather than going to individuals (the all-important second greeting), then my stress would have become their stress. The consistency of the greeting helped everyone know that all would be okay. And it was. These first and second moments of service told the guests that they could be a passenger and enjoy their time at the Plaza Hotel.

Your Way

There are many unique ways to greet your guests and customers. What is your place of business? Make sure your greeting sets the tone for an appropriate experience as this moment of service, whether on the phone or in person, has great power to set up expectations. At the radiologist's office, for instance, the tone should be warm and respectful and reassure the patients that they will be treated with care. The greeting must not in any way sound abrupt or rude or send the wrong message about care, about timing of an appointment, or about reliability. It could be "Hello! Who are you here to see today?" or "Hi! May I have your name to check your appointment information?" At so many medical offices these days there is no greeting whatsoever. There is merely a sign-in sheet that has boxes to check (payment and insurance information) and a box to indicate arrival time and time of appointment next to the patient's name. What a cold way to start this important relationship! The time boxes can shame patients if they are a minute late, and the payment information (cash or credit card)—which is nobody's business—is now public, visible to all the other patients arriving later in the day. The values of discretion and care are lost at this important point in patients' arrival and sets them on a course of discomfort. This is a discomfort patients have become all too familiar with.

Often when a receptionist answer the phone, the requisite greeting is "doctor's office." This tells me, as a patient, nothing. Did I reach the right place? Is my doctor even at this office? Have I reached a switchboard, or can I launch into describing my ailment to this stranger? These are too many questions for any first-time caller to have to deal with. But this problem is not unique to medical offices; indeed, very often the actual greeting has been sacrificed for a description of the office reached, for example, "X, Y, Z attorneys," "ABC Auto," or even a cheery declaration "Cut and Dry Sa-lo-on!" These are not greetings; they are statements. These statements do nothing to invite customers in, and they keep customers in the dark, unsure about whether they can start their dialogue with this person on the phone. And if customers dare to start asking something, they may get another statement in return: "Please hold," "Debbie's at lunch, call back after 2," or "I'm sorry we're booked that day." These also do nothing to further the relationship with the client or to create a repeat guest.

Adding some authentic niceties costs nothing extra. Go on, toss in a salutation! "Hello," "Hi," "Good afternoon," and even "Howdy" are all decent conversation starters. And this is truly the simplest way to start adding some warmth and personality to this moment of service. Some businesses do this very well; they infuse their personality and brand into every conversation with their guests, on the phone and in person.

No one does this better than Zappos. Zappos is not only a huge retailer but also a huge proponent of delivering excellent service. The executives at Zappos truly understand that their staff delivers the service that is so renowned, and they have created core values that are the heart and soul of the business. Tony Hsieh, the CEO, has said that the executives developed the core values of the company by surveying the team and spending a year getting the values just right. These core values are something the company lives by. In a video interview on the Inc.com website titled "Tony Hsieh: I Fire Those Who Don't Fit Our Company Culture" Hsieh says that even if an employee is "a superstar at their job, if they're bad for our culture, then we will fire them for that reason alone." The company is that serious about its core values, and these values shape the workplace, the culture, and the relationship of the employees to the brand and to their customers.

The core values inspire the "Zappos greeting" and in a YouTube video called "How to Answer the Telephone the Zappos Way," the company leaders advise new employees that "the key to answering the phone the Zappos way is having a smile in your voice [and] having a good tone of voice so the customer can hear how excited you are [to be at] work." The tutorial shows several employees using creativity and a little zaniness to answer the phone in unique and friendly ways. One staff member calls himself a "Zappo-potamus"; another answers the call with "It's a Zapp-tastic day here at Zappos.com; how may I help you?" This brings the company's core values[1] to life, for example, value #1 ("Deliver 'wow' through service") or value #3 ("Create fun and a little weirdness"). With each call the core values are being expressed, and the customer knows exactly what the service experience will be like at this unique and successful company.

The culture and core values of Zappos directs the style of the "Zappos greeting" and makes it authentic to the Zappos brand. It is essential that your greeting is authentic to you and your business. Your greeting is a big part of your brand identity, and it can verbally represent your brand personality and embody your mission, ethos, credo, vision, and core values. What is great about establishing service as an intrinsic piece of your business is that part of your vision will be lived out every moment of the day each time a staff member greets a customer. There are various businesses that include service as part of their core values. The US Air Force has three core values, the second of them is "Service before Self." The guiding principle of J. C. Penney, originally called the Golden Rule in 1902, addresses service quite simply: "Do unto others as you would have others do unto you."

The examples above show how to make service and the customer experience part of a company's core values or mission. Each of these companies knows that this simple but essential focus on customers and their experience is the key to their success. Why doesn't every major brand do this? To some corporations such practices might seem rather silly: they are in business to create and keep customers, why should they have to state the obvious? Many people would call this common sense. But is common sense common? Nope, it is not. You have to create the common sense for your business and build a language of common sense by working on every moment of the customer experience. It is not silly, and it is not exactly easy, but it will be worth your while.

Virtual Reality

The greeting happens with real people, but it also happens on your website. How are your guests acknowledged when they want to learn more about your products and services? Many websites have a welcome page, which offers an opportunity to connect to browsing clients in a unique way. For example, the welcome page can be the first page your clients see, and many great websites invite their visitors to explore, discover, or learn more about the people and products that make the brand unique and the website indispensable.

Your website should demonstrate your brand personality and make your guests feel welcome and invited into your brand, your culture, and your online world. The whole purpose of a good website is to keep people engaged with your business, help them maximize their experience of your business, and keep them interested as long as possible.

When you set up a website, you will use reference tools called web analytics. With web analytics you will learn how the public is using and finding your site. One of the first things to look at to see if your website is successful is the bounce rate. The bounce rate tells you how long people remain on your site before leaving. A high bounce rate means that people are leaving your site without lingering, and a low bounce rate means that people stay engaged on your site, exploring more pages, or reading more content. Most businesses try to optimize their websites in order to reduce the bounce rate. Google, one of the main providers of web analytics, has a list of only three reasons for a high bounce rate, and the first reason is a faulty or ineffective welcome page (or landing page). According to the Google Analytics help page, if you get this wrong, then your potential customers bounce off your site before entering or learning more about your products and services. If you have a high bounce rate, you must consider your digital greeting. How are you presenting your business to first-time customers? This landing page or welcome page is the difference between increased sales and flat sales, and this virtual greeting is at the heart of it all.

The good thing about a virtual greeting is that it is always the same. Likewise, you want some consistency if your greeting is face-to-face or live on the phone with a real person. Often, businesses create scripts for employees to follow that demonstrate how best to talk about products and services and how to talk to customers. This is a great way to formulate the path toward understanding a product or a process, but there is an inherent challenge: the person answering the phone should not sound like a robot. The classic scripted experience is that of a cold call. People calling a potential customer's number and launching into a spiel about why the person on the other end needs their product or service or why he or she should donate money to their cause. We have all received calls like this. The scripts are unrelenting in their tone and delivery of content; scripts are created in order to bombard the person called with as much information as possible before he or she hangs up. In my experience cold calls allow no time for breaks to register whether the potential customer is actually engaged in the phone call. The greeting is glossed over and becomes social "roadkill," rolled over without any thought. For example, the caller might say, "Good evening, how are you, I'm calling because of the plight of the walrus; did you know that...." Of course, with such a caller I want to get off the phone immediately; the caller is talking at me, not to me or with me.

When people call a business, they want information or solutions to their problems. When the greeting and additional verbiage sound canned or inauthentic, that is a huge turnoff. You don't want to turn off your customers; you want to turn them into repeat guests. So create a simple script or "road map" for your greeting and initial conversation, and then have your employees practice using the road map as a guide for how they would naturally talk to a potential customer on the phone. If the scripted greeting is "Thank you for calling Acme Auto Supply. We appreciate your business; how can we can help you today?" you may encourage your team members to use the key concepts (Acme Auto Supply/appreciation/what can I do?) but to say the rest in their own words. One person may say, "This is Acme Auto Supply; so glad you called; how may I help you?" Another employee might say, "Good morning! We appreciate that you called Acme; how may I direct your call?" The more authentic your team can sound, the more your message will register as truthful with your customers. And truth is at the heart of it all.

In addition, it is important to note that "hello" is not just verbal but vocal. How you say it is as important or even more important than what you say. Paralanguage, as defined by Wikipedia, is the way you say a word; the inflections, tone of voice, and volume used as you deliver a verbal message. Nuances of emotion are expressed through paralanguage. Exasperation is expressed with a huff, impatience with a click of the tongue, boredom with a long exhalation. We all express our feelings this way; it is a fantastic human feature, but in your business you must be aware that these numerous little cues can impact the greeting and color the impression customers have of your service and staff.

It is possible to say "may I help you?" in a dozen different ways just by playing with your voice; you create changes in meaning with each adjustment. You can demonstrate enthusiasm when saying "may I help you?" by placing an emphasis on the "oo" sounds and giving an upward inflection that signals a question. This enthusiastic tone can go a long way when the energy, posture, and eye contact accompanying the words are also in sync and are authentic to the speaker. It transmits sincerity and demonstrates that your question is not in passing; you are genuine in your concern and care. You want your guests to feel your true intentions; anything less than sincere will come across as false and this is the antithesis of good service.

People can spot a fake. They can sense insincerity. Empowering your team to take ownership of the script helps eliminate these concerns. As humans, we often ridicule people who appear insincere or phony thus you never want your staff members to look or sound insincere. The phrase "how are you doing?" can sound insincere all too quickly. "How are you doing?" has all but replaced "hello" as a greeting even though it has become a colloquial question that requires no response. Most of the time when someone asks "how are you doing?" the common response is "hey" or "how are you doing?" This is a total fake-out: the asker really has no interest in a reply, and it becomes a mock greeting that does little to invite further conversation.

So, what is your mission? What are your core values? Do they include service and interaction with your guests as a way to reflect your brand identity? Now you can formulate an authentic and welcoming greeting that will touch all of your guests, remotely and in person. And once you have created the greeting and trained your staff on the greeting you're all done with this moment of service, right? You have set up an expectation, and now you ask that everyone meet it. But the truth is that your employees won't meet it if they are not sure what the expectation is; they simply cannot. Therefore, it is your duty to create and uphold your expectations every moment of every day. If you are diligent about living the mission and values of your business and you insist that your staff do so as well, then you will have the opportunity to achieve your mission, achieve your goals for your business, and achieve the service that impacts your guests in a positive way. And yes, it is that easy.

Tips and Takeaways

- **Be the First**. As a manager or leader you must be the first to say "hello" to the staff and to greet your customers. You can lift the spirits of your team members as they start their day by greeting them, asking about their morning, or checking in on their progress with a project or client. Your leadership and your positive energy will help buoy the team throughout the day. Remember: service is all about a conversation, so if you can start one with your team members, you will grease the wheels of friendliness and get them ready to serve with a smile.

- **Internal Hello**. Make sure that your greeting standards are also echoed and utilized internally as well. I always say that it is hard speaking to strangers, so we must "warm up" by connecting with someone we know first. Your greeting is your first point of engagement with your staff. Use an internal greeting (stopping to say hello and give a handshake or a high five) that helps to warm your team members up and get them ready for a productive workday engaging your customers and clients.

- **Yo**. Your greeting can be a differentiator. Get creative and think about the ways your business "greets" your customers and potential clients in person but also in written and online communication. The way you reach out to your clients can be a unique reminder of your brand and the experience that you stand for.

- **Embodying Hello**. As you read through this book, you will notice that there are many themes that crop up. "Hello" is one of them, and how you say it makes all the difference. Consider your body language and what that transmits when you are greeting your team. Consider your vocal color as you speak the words "good morning"—do you sound like you think it is a good day indeed? Check out chapter 12 for more tips and takeaways about how your poise and professionalism can inspire your team and your guests.

CHAPTER 2

I Notice = I Care

I Spy

Carolyn Paddock has been in corporate and commercial aviation for 25 years. During her time in the business, she has flown everyone from international pop stars and top-tier actors to billionaires and members of the Saudi Royal family. The service she delivers is in keeping with this exceptional mode of travel; she works with her passengers in a luxury environment that is relatively small and incredibly intimate. This is not a job for the faint of heart, as she must deliver a customized experience within the strictest of standards of passenger safety and bespoke customer service.

On an overnight flight where the sofas were made up into beds, Carolyn noticed that one of her passengers frequently got into bed only to get up a bit later to take a call or get a drink of water. At these times she would go and straighten the sheets, as she wanted his bed to look perfect when he returned. Each time he returned his bed was remade and looked fresh and tidy; he clearly liked this attention to detail. Carolyn, however, noticed a small, but important point; when returning to bed he frequently had something in his hand, whether it was a glass of water or his phone. This made pulling back the tucked-in sheets a little more difficult and not as quick as if he had returned to an unmade bed, and so Carolyn made a correction. Rather than tucking in the sheets, she straightened the covers and folded back the top so there was an inviting "opening" for the passenger to use. Rather than having to pull apart a freshly made bed, all he had to do was slip right in. Easy to do, this action and correction showed Carolyn's consideration for her passenger.

What Carolyn did was notice. And when she acted on what she had noticed, her passenger felt cared for, and care means everything in the customer service relationship. As business owners or managers, your job is to care for those in your businesses, but "caring" for strangers is not as easy as it sounds. Why? Because you can't make your staff actually feel for your customers. But you can ask your employees to notice what is happening to their customers (a customer entering the business) and empower them to act on what they see (I'll open the door for this person), and your customer, in turn, will feel cared for, nurtured, and considered (what a thoughtful gesture). With each action you let the guest know that you noticed. Each time you noticed you acted, demonstrating to your guests that you were fully aware of their situation. Noticing their individual situation let them feel cared for. It's that simple: observe the situation and offer an action.

My principle of "I notice = I care" gives everyone involved in the service equation what they want. It gives guests the "care" they seek while giving staff members concrete things to do to demonstrate care for their guests. This is a surefire way to get positive feedback. With the "I notice = I care" equation, everyone wins.

It is actually easier to understand the principle of "I notice = I care" by looking at things from the opposite direction. Most people perceive inattentive service as the staff "not caring," and this is a very clear equation as well: I didn't notice = I didn't care. Or from the guests' perspective: "no one notices me/my situation = no one here cares at all." Ouch. But this is really the way it feels. For example, customers will remember the frustration of waiting on hold on the phone (no one notices I'm patiently waiting = no one cares about my time) or of getting an overstuffed shopping bag that is about to break (the salesperson didn't notice that this bag is overstuffed = he doesn't care about getting everything home in one piece) or of struggling to exit the kids' store while managing a baby, a stroller, a bag, and another child and the staff lingers nearby chatting (those employees didn't notice my struggle = they don't give a hoot). As a business owner or manager, this is not what you want your customers to think and remember. Your customers should never wonder whether your company cares about them as customers or as people. Even if customers assume that big business is a cold, dark, and inhuman force, your job is to show some hospitality to your customers every time.

The term "hospitality" deserves some attention, as it is a challenging idea for our business-oriented minds. Generally, "hospitality" and "business" are distant cousins—or are they? Many people have notions about big business: cutthroat corporate villains driven by the bottom line, focused on getting ahead at any cost. And "hospitality" almost seems like a picture out of the 1950s: sugary smiling staff, outstretched hands, saccharin slogans like "We're here for you!" In fact, however, the best-run and most successful businesses are very focused on their customers and their staff, and thus they epitomize the essence of hospitality.

"Hospitality" is defined by the *New Oxford American Dictionary*, as "the friendly and generous reception and entertainment of guests, visitors, or strangers." One usually associates hospitality with the restaurant or hotel business, but in truth it really defines what many businesses do daily. No matter what the business is, it receives any number of people a day; its success depends on both the first-timers and the repeat guests. A business is friendly and generous with its time and approach. It is there to provide an experience (aka: entertain) with what it offers to its customers. And businesses offer their experience to guests (the name for our clients, who, we hope, will be repeat guests), visitors (one-time guests), and strangers (first-time guests). [Throughout the book I will use "guests," "customers," and "clients" interchangeably. One may apply more to your business but all are meant to represent the people who you rely on to patronize your business.]

Customer service is all about thinking of your customers' needs, and this is where the associations with hospitality have their roots. "Thinking of your guests' needs" is very close to "caring" for your guests, and while managers and staff members do it all the time, it is impossible to ask someone to care. Either the person cares or doesn't. Many businesses work very hard to try and hire people who have a caring nature. There are online surveys designed to decode whether the applicant has the "caring gene" or not. There are scripted interview questionnaires written to allow interviewers to determine whether the applicant is more likely to be empathetic or self-centered. And while well-meaning and basically effective, the business of service can be quite relentless and hard to do. In any customer service position you are dealing with strangers day in and day out, and the personalities and moods of your customers require an emotional fortitude that takes time to build and finesse. Even the most qualified and caring pro will be put to the test when engaging with an especially difficult customer. There are few questionnaires that can determine how an applicant will act under duress.

Therefore, what I look for in an applicant is a high level of empathy combined with high energy and an interest in "doing." Customer service requires boundless energy; staff members must always be "on" and must be aware of their surroundings and the customers in their business. So I look for people who will be active and who can demonstrate through their actions that they are by nature empathetic. While "being empathetic" can be draining, "acting on what you see" can be fun. Here's the difference: instead of feeling like you have to ask "How are you today?" to show interest in a guest who is looking around, you can offer "May I get you a basket?" as you see that the customer does not have one. To sound authentic, "How are you today?" must convey care and concern, that is, empathetic. And that is a lot to ask of a staff member. Offering a basket or offering to show the customer an item or area of the business utilizes energy and knowledge. And *demonstrates* empathy. The empathy is secondary to the action, but the action itself demonstrates care. This focus on energetic observation is key to the customer experience, and it is at the core of my principle "I notice = I care." Hiring staff with energy combined with empathy is a little easier than finding someone who is only empathetic. Give me someone with empathy and energy any day— empathy alone won't do the job.

Don't get me wrong. You must seek out individuals with an outwardly empathetic nature. But when it comes time to ask your employees to "be empathetic," asking is a little harder to do. Empathy takes a lot of emotional energy, and while it can feel very rewarding, empathy is not always rewarded. In every job we all like to know (and are inspired to work harder) when our efforts have made a difference.

In the hospitality business there is a convention known as "reading the guest." "Reading the guest" means observing the cues the customer is giving and then reacting to what is observed. For example, when a cashier is "reading" that someone has her hands full as she is checking out at the register, the cashier might ask this customer whether she has a car outside or needs help getting a cab. This starts a conversation and demonstrates the care that the customer might not be expecting but will certainly appreciate. "Reading the guest" is really asking you to be tuned in, to understand and consider your guest while you are "taking care" of him or her. But it is much easier and more business-like to ask your staff to use their empathy by "reading" someone rather than to instruct them to "be empathetic." And it is easier to ask someone to look for cues to respond to than to ask the person to "care about" a virtual stranger.

There is a children's guessing game called "I Spy." It is an easy game that starts with a little rhyme, "I spy with my little eye," and then one child finds and focuses on an object and invites another to guess what the object is by asking yes/no questions. For example, if the first child says "I spy with my little eye…something blue," the other child will ask a series of questions (Is it on the floor? Is it made of plastic? Is it round? Is it the dog dish?) in order to guess what that "something blue" is. The first child can respond with "yes" or "no" or with "hot" or "cold" to indicate that the guesser is closer to getting it right or is going in the wrong direction. The game is a great way to explore your surroundings and focus on the little details around you while passing the time.

Asking your employees to notice everything that is happening with your customers is a bit like "I Spy" in that you are asking them to focus on little details and act on what they see. It is essential to show the team what to notice and how to act on it. Sometimes noticing could result in a conversation ("May I help you with your things?"), or an action (helping someone open the door to enter a business), or an appearance (making eye contact to show that you are there and able to help). All these are actions that tell guests that you see them and their situation and are able to help. Noticing all the little things is a key component in the customer service equation.

When working with any type of full-service restaurant, I always ask the staff to help people with their chairs. Both men and women appreciate someone who comes to help with their chair, it is an age-old custom, and it really impresses people. And here's the secret: you don't even have to get there in time. Just the fact that you came across the room to make an effort to be there demonstrated that you noticed the guest has arrived at the table. And even when the guest in question doesn't see that you are there to help pull or push in his chair, you can bet that the others at the table did see. You made an effort to demonstrate that you noticed and that is appreciated. This is just one example of many "things to notice and act on that will really impress your guests." What you do can be big or small, but it adds up. Simple things, such as holding a door when a guest enters or leaves, pushing an elevator button before the client goes to that floor, calling to confirm a reservation rather than asking the guest to do so, are easy to do and demonstrate clearly that you notice the customers' experience.

We all notice things "with our little eye." Sometimes we are focusing precisely on a particular thing. Sometimes what we are looking at is secondary to our thought at the moment. But either way, we have observed this thing, this object, this event, and it has now become a thought, however small, that can inspire a memory.

Memories...

Our memory is like a sieve; every moment of every experience gets passed through our memory, and various pieces of the experience stick. Memory is made up of three stages: encoding (grasping what you are experiencing and putting it into thought), storage (how we store thoughts and access them, both short-term and long-term storage), and retrieval (accessing that thought). The first part, encoding, is making sense of what you are experiencing; we do this visually, acoustically, or through semantics or meaning. Then we have to figure out how to organize this thought: is it something to be accessed quickly or accessed after a longer period of time? Our brain will determine whether the information that is coming in will go to short-term or to long-term memory. Short-term memory only exists for 30 seconds or less, and we can only store between seven and nine thoughts at one time during this period; thoughts go into short-term memory and are immediately pushed out again by other thoughts coming in after the first ones. Long-term memory is considered to be unlimited; thoughts can exist there for a lifetime.

We retrieve our thoughts from short-term memory and long-term memory quite differently. Memories stored in short-term memory are retrieved sequentially, what went in first will always be first when we refer to it again. A sequence of numbers (for example, 1, 10, 25, 45) will always be accessed in that same sequence (rather than as 10, 25, 1, 45). But long-term memories are retrieved in a different way: by association. Where you were, who you were with, what the weather was like when you first had the thought will be remembered and will remain attached to the memory forever. We are reminded of things that have been stored in long-term memory when we return to locations we know or when we see old friends. We get flooded with memories when we see a childhood toy or a familiar object or place. These associations are very strong; they have attached to our thoughts, were stored in our memory, and stay attached to the thought forever.

One of my clearest childhood memories is the scent of my grandmother's new shower curtain. Fresh green vinyl, just out of the package, hung in her new apartment bathroom still ripe with the scent of polymers and plastic. Just smelling anything like it transports me back in time. My grandmother had just moved into an apartment on the ground floor of a newish complex about a mile from our home. In my mind, the mind of a ten-year-old, this was the coolest, most amazing possibility: one could live in a one-bedroom home on one floor with everything in close proximity. It was like a little piece of heaven, and it was the first time I was introduced to the idea of apartment living (a cozy home), female independence (my grandmother was living alone for the first time), and freedom of choice (that green shower curtain, divine!). My memory of the scent of the shower curtain is just the portal to many powerful feelings: the associations and the emotions they inspire are way bigger than the scent of the shower curtain alone.

We all have experiences like this. Our memories create associations laced with emotions and strong feelings. And while my memory was wonderful and filled with associations of possibility, some memories are not so great but are equally powerful. Think about the last glass door that you opened when entering a store or bank. Was the glass clean or covered in fingerprints? How about that chair in the waiting room? Was it a little wobbly, a little sticky? How about the subway or bus? Grimy and never cleaned? In all of these situations you will remember something but not about entering a building, meeting a colleague, or getting to work. Instead, you have taken in moments that have left memories of cleanliness and care. Things someone else failed to notice and act on.

Associations are powerful carriers of emotion. Our memories inspire associations, emotions, and reactions in us that are complex and dynamic. And creating memories and associations is what business is all about. Madison Avenue execs have gotten rich by making use of associations in every ad in print, on TV or on a billboard. Just the sound of a popping soda can cap inspires thirst! The picture of sizzling meat can make us feel hungry. There are many such associations businesses depend on to make sales.

People will remember many things about your business. They will remember the things you have actively presented to them about your business and they will remember many other things that they noticed on their own. They will create many associations that will attach to these memories about their experience in your business. And then they will perceive your business based on their memories and associations. Perception is reality. So even if your business delivers an experience with service that shines (the line was short; that one salesperson was so helpful; I found exactly what I needed), your customers will have associations with each moment that shape their perception of their experience and your business (the line was short, and I was standing under an a/c vent; that salesperson had a tattoo with a Japanese character; I found what I needed, and Beyoncé was playing in the background). They will remember this experience and your business because of the associations they made. This is a win-win situation. Your business demonstrated that it noticed the customer, and the customer felt cared for and remembers this positive impression.

But what if everything happened as above, but on the way out the guest notices a pile of returned items sitting next to the last register? What will your customer be thinking? "What happens to that stuff? Does it go back on a shelf? Is *my* stuff used? I hope not." In short, every little thing people notice represents an opportunity for them to trust your business or doubt it. When *you* notice all the little things in your business (there is a pile of returns at register 12) and act on what you see (let's return it to the stock room ASAP), then there is little left to impact your customers' memories other than what you intend them to experience. Their reality is then your reality: because you made it so. That means that you must be prepared: prepared to notice everything.

This opens up a Pandora's box of "things to notice" about your business. Your guests will notice everything about your business, and this means you have to notice *first*. One thing I always look for when asked to assess a new client's business is dust. Is there dust on the plants, speakers, columns, picture frames, lighting fixtures, and venting louvers? Businesses where managers or staff have noticed this and have cleaned it, demonstrate "I notice" to me and everyone else who may be looking around. In your business "I notice" extends to cleanliness but also to every detail under your roof. The temperature of your space, the sounds, the smells, and even the lighting all contribute to the guests' overall impression. Every little thing that someone will experience on an emotional or physical level is something that you must notice and react to. Service-oriented businesses are all about noticing guests and anticipating their needs. And by demonstrating that you notice, you are demonstrating to your guests that you care about them, their patronage, and their comfort. The service experience is not just about service; it is about action, intervention, and communication. And if you can act, intervene, and communicate with your guests, then you have a great chance of surviving and succeeding on many levels for years to come.

You Smell Marvelous

Being proactive is part of "noticing" your guests and their experience. A great number of businesses focus on the odor of their public spaces and spend millions on creating a signature scent for their business. Hotels are the leaders in this area and are proactive about the customer experience, down to the scent of the lobby. In New York City, the Gramercy Park Hotel has partnered with La Labo, a high-end British fragrance company, to design a signature scent for the hotel. When you walk into the hotel, the scent is there: familiar, complex, noticeable, and intoxicating. WestHouse hotel in Manhattan invested in a custom fragrance for the hotel called "Guests Only" and designed by a fragrance company called 12.29 that designs bespoke "olfactory identities" for its clients (including fashion designer Jason Wu and auto manufacturer Mercedes Benz).

So why spend money on a signature scent? Well, let's go back to memory and association: our olfactory system is said to be 10,000 times more sensitive than sight, taste, and hearing. Our sense of smell activates an intense memory of a business that will remain in our minds—with powerful positive associations. Giving a business a signature scent is a proactive way to create a memory that people will associate with a warm welcome, an exclusive experience, or a beautiful setting. Being proactive is what service is about, creating a signature scent and utilizing it in your customer areas is just one way to demonstrate that you notice and care about the customers' experience.

Because our sense of smell is so very strong, it is important to consider all the aspects of scent in your business. Some unassuming businesses are known for their inherent scent: a cobbler smells like leather and polish; a bakery smells of yeast, caramel, and vanilla; a flower shop smells of, you guessed it, roses and lilies. So what if your business smells like something unexpected? Imagine an office that smells of chlorine, a cheese store that smells of Windex, or a dentist's office that smells of a wet mop. These, too, create associations and will impact the customers' experience.

Service as a whole is active and intentional. When unintentional events occur (my appointment is running late; the item I ordered is wrong), customers say that "the service was bad." Unintended things occurred and this tilts the scale of service from "intentionally good" to "unintentionally bad" and then straight into "bad service." These unintended moments are the sort of memory that people keep and ponder over long after experiencing bad service. The memory has been created, and the customer now has the resulting feelings. But in fact, the bad *unintended* memories (my steak was completely overcooked) stick just as easily as the positive *intended* recovery (so they sent us a round of drinks), and this latter action becomes a memory as well. The memories of good service, of positive intentional actions, are indelible.

It is important to recognize that you are providing an experience for your guests, one that will make them feel cared for and inspire them to come back. Every little thing in your business will inspire a memory of your brand. So you must be proactive, alert, and attentive to everything that the customer may experience. You must do everything possible in order to create a positive impression so that your business stays in your customers' memories for all the right reasons.

Tips and Takeaways

- **You First**. Noticing starts with you, the manager or leader. When you walk by things that are out of place or when you fail to notice something that a staff member is doing, then you send the message that it is okay to turn a blind eye to the workplace and staff. You must uphold the brand by acting in its best interest. Noticing and acting on what you notice is important to your success as a leader; you will come across as being able to "see everything," which keeps your employees on their toes. It also sends the message to the guests who are around you that you don't miss a beat and that the operation is running well under your supervision.
- **Share What You See**. You must train your employees to notice the little things and to act on what they see. Leading by example is a positive way to demonstrate many important things, but you must also encourage the team members to act on what they notice as well. Ask your team for feedback about your space and work environment, ask them what they observe in serving their guests and clients, and ask them for creative solutions to what they observe. Your team is made up of many individuals who have the power to notice and care about your guests. Allow them to also notice and care about your business; it is their workplace after all, and little improvements can go a long way toward developing a satisfied team.
- **Notice Your Team**. The principle of "I notice = I care" applies also to seeing your staff members and engaging with them in a positive way. You can engage with your teams by noticing what they do and need and then acting on it as well. Innovate new ways to "notice" things about

your business. For example, you can design a contest that involves the team in making improvements to the space you all share or the systems you all use. Awards such as "employee of the month" can be made more unique to your brand and fun for the staff when you highlight a new way of looking at things in your business. And by noticing and acknowledging the people who notice things, you are also demonstrating that you care about your employees.

- **Connect with Your Guests.** I've coached new managers who have trouble finding ways to talk to or connect to guests except when there is a problem. They have trouble just walking up to a customer and engaging; it is hard to do and most managers are fearful of intruding on the guests' experience. If you want to engage with your customers, apply the principle of "I notice = I care" to create ways of connecting. Have your new manager posted near the front of your store and offer shopping baskets or have the manager ask customers whether they know in what aisle to find what they are looking for. By noticing that the customer may need assistance, the manager has an opportunity to interact with the patron in a way that can potentially lead to a natural conversation. Help set your new managers up for success by talking through good opportunities to notice guests in your business. This way you can get new managers more comfortable in their role and help them gain confidence in speaking with customers.

CHAPTER 3

The Power of Chairs, Doors, and Stairs

So Many Choices

After paying over a billion dollars to purchase and renovate the historic landmark hotel where Truman Capote staged his Black and White Ball and where the Beatles stayed during their first American tour, the last thing the new owners of The Plaza Hotel expected was to be derailed by their choice of chairs. But in fact, chairs contributed to the downfall of the 2008 version of The Palm Court at The Plaza Hotel.

They aren't just any chairs. They were luxurious blue velvet, regal and in keeping with the grandeur of this storied hotel. Unfortunately, they were clunky and awkward and were so uncomfortable that they were included in a restaurant review by Ryan Sutton, published on the Bloomberg website. In his review he described them as "throne-like chairs so high they block [your view]. They also provide no lumbar support; your back will hurt by mid-meal."[1] The unwieldy and uncomfortable chairs colored his otherwise positive review.

I remember dining there and the poor host being completely unable to pull out or push in my chair. It took a number of servers to push in my chair (I felt like Eloise), and then when I had the desire to get up and wash my hands, I found myself practically trapped by the size and weight of this behemoth. Then came the service of the table. Just to serve from the left and clear from the right became a joke as the servers could barely get their arms around half the seat back. I remember a server trying to do the right thing by performing the tableside service of pouring hollandaise over my eggs Benedict, but he was precariously stuck between my chair and the one behind me; it was a close to disastrous moment. Service was forced to take a backseat: there simply wasn't any room for anyone to move.

If feeling awkward and trapped wasn't bad enough, the clincher was the height of the seat backs, which prevented guests from seeing anyone else in the dining room. This took all the people-watching fun—the main reason many people paid up to $100 a person for afternoon tea—from dining at The Palm Court. I wasn't surprised when The Palm Court closed again for renovations and replacement chairs. In truth, chairs can make or break you.

You must come to grips with one essential concept before opening a business: every choice you make will affect your guests. That's right; everything in your business will have an impact on your customers' experience. Sounds far-reaching but it is true. As customers, we are impacted by many facets of a business: the layout (is it easy to navigate?), the doors (do you push or pull them?), the chairs (are they comfortable?), the signage (easy to read and understand?), the bathroom (is it clean and does it assure privacy?), the pen (does it display an inappropriate-to-your-business pharmaceutical brand name?), the stairs (are they safe to traverse?), and all the décor. And at each point of contact with each one of your choices you help create an image for your guest, one that will stay with the guest's memory of your business, good or bad. And all of these tactile pieces of your business—doors, walls, chairs, floors, light switches, pens, receipts, and more—are not just objects. They are emotional touchpoints that have the real power to draw in or drive away your customers.

Touchy-Feely

Our sense of touch is a gateway to powerful emotions. From a young age we want to touch everything we come in contact with. As parents of toddlers know, little kids will touch, pick up, and handle everything they come in contact with; touching is an innate way to experience the world and gather information. As we mature, touch is a sense we come to rely on in our day-to-day life. People choose clothes by stroking the fabric with their fingers; most chefs can tell if meat is cooked medium rare or medium well by feeling the resistance of each steak; musicians play instruments, and the touch of their fingers is all it takes to create incredible sound. We touch everything, and these things, in turn, touch us.

Marketers are beginning to capitalize on the power of touch in selling products and services. In an article posted on the *Harvard Business Review* website titled "Please Touch the Merchandise" Lawrence Williams and Joshua Ackerman make the case that "physically holding products can create a sense of psychological ownership, driving must-have purchase decisions."[2] This is why electronic products are now displayed in the open instead of in secure cases. The executives at Apple and Best Buy understand that touch is the sense that actually makes the sale. The displays, products, and demos are the things they are inviting their customers to come into contact with.

But what about the things people are touching that are a bit more indirect? The point of sale kiosk used to swipe your credit card (is it functional and does the screen register the signature?), the elevator (are the buttons worn down; are the numbers legible?), the waiting room magazine (has it been wrinkled from overuse and are pages missing?), and the dreaded sign-in sheet (is the pen attached to the clipboard by a string of rubber bands and some scotch tape?)— all these make impressions, not because customers see them, but because they touch them. Touching fast-tracks that experience straight into our long-term memory where it attaches itself to thoughts of your business.

New information about our sense of touch is still being discovered. A fascinating study was conducted to see how different experiences utilizing touch (weight, hardness, and texture) yield various outcomes. The researchers recorded their findings in a study entitled "Incidental Haptic Sensations Influence Social Judgments and Decisions."[3] In one experiment they divided car buyers into two groups and seated one group in hard, uncomfortable chairs and the other in soft, cushiony chairs. Guess which buyers were more inclined to open up their wallets? If you guess the people who were made more comfortable spent more money, you're right. Meanwhile the people in uncomfortable chairs spent 28 percent less for the new car than the people sitting in comfy chairs. In other words, the harder the chair, the harder the sale. In another experiment volunteers were given a resume on either a hard and heavy clipboard or on a flimsy and light one. Those who held the heavier clipboard registered the resume as more impressive than the volunteers seeing the same resume on the flimsy clipboard. Similarly, when people were given mineral water to drink, the ones who got it in sturdy cups rated the water as better than did those who got it in flimsy containers. Touch will either enhance the customers' experience, inspire them to buy more and take you seriously, or it will do the opposite.

Small touches can be the most powerful. One gracious gesture that capitalized on the power of touch was demonstrated the last time I was at the podiatrist. The people on staff gave me little paper slippers to wear once I took off my shoes while in the examining room. When the doctor examined my feet, he removed them gently in a reverse Cinderella moment. Offering a slipper made me feel respected: the employees assumed I did not want to walk barefoot through their office. The consideration that this action transmits to patients goes a long way and makes a statement that no laminated sign can convey: we care about our patients.

Another tactile gesture is to offer your guests a hot cup of tea or coffee. It turns out that warmth engenders warmth from your guests. That's right. Researchers at Yale found that subjects holding a warm cup of coffee rated the person they were speaking with as more open and warm.[4] Researchers call this "priming,"[5] a process in which one sensation opens the door to more similar sensations. The flip side is also true, and in the study those who were given a cold cup to hold had cooler feelings about the person they were with. So how are you "priming" your guests? What are your guests coming into contact with in your business? You must be aware of just what might be priming them and what they are touching, feeling, and using; each thing customers use has a weight they feel.

The Physical—and the Virtual—Aspects of Comfort

One of the biggest and expansive human states is comfort. How people feel when they are in contact with your business is an important feeling to understand. Comfort can make or break a sale and can potentially lose you customers before they ever get close to spending money. Comfort and ease in your space even has an impact on the Internet. For example, my decision to buy has often been influenced by a website that looked amateurish, slapped together, confusing, slow, and too many flash animations that offered outdated content. Websites that are hard to navigate are frustrating for users and will likely turn them away from your products because they cannot easily figure out how to make a purchase. The best businesses go back, evaluate, evolve, and listen to critical customer feedback because they know customers' comfort matters.

Comfort manifests itself in many ways in the physical world of your business, for example, that door your customers can't tell whether to push or pull, the bathroom that is not clearly marked for men or women, that unique shopping bag that is an unwieldy size and hard to manage, seating that is way too low or uncomfortable. These are all making impressions on your paying customers and will stay in their memories and potentially keep them from returning. Look at those shops that favor form over function: they are unique and sleek but their design is hard to understand, unwieldy, uncomfortable, and hard to connect to. Form over function is a great mantra but be warned: you must constantly work to maintain this look. I had a client who invested in iconic bentwood chairs that cost $2,400 per chair. You should have seen when a full-sized adult male tried to extricate himself from it: the creaking and groaning of the chair was worrisome for both the business and the customer. Both wondered if it was going to break. Beautiful design is wonderful, but whether the fixture is $2,400 or $24, make sure it does not interfere with the overall comfort and experience of the guest. Remember that what you're aiming for is comfort, that state of ease where everything feels in perfect balance.

Comfort is also a feeling that will bring people back to your business and inspire folks to share their opinion of your business with others. Comfort in your business is the first way to invite people to become "regulars." Regular guests are what every business strives to cultivate, guests who return again and again become our highest spenders over months and years. Part of being a regular is that pride in knowing and feeling at home in a business. This pride allows for people to share in your success, and this is the true value: regulars will be on your side and will talk up your business to others. They will also demonstrate pride of ownership by introducing the business to their friends and colleagues. It feels wonderful when you are remembered at a place you frequent and then introduce the business to another person. It demonstrates that the regular is a memorable patron, not just a "regular Joe" and that this introduction is actually worth something. It is collateral that has meaning.

Regulars are complex characters. They are the ones that come regularly to your business: often, they know you better than you know yourselves. In terms of building sales, your regulars are a great asset, and they can also help you know your business better. In my experience, regulars will tell you when you are doing things well or when you have dropped the ball. Regulars will also become proprietary about your stuff. In restaurants regulars want certain tables ("my table," they call it); in retail it may be that they only talk to one person ("my guy" at the store is their go-to person); in sales it might be speaking to the head, director, or manager ("my service" is handled by only one person, that person at the top.) Let the regulars take ownership; this allows them to become a part of your business, and they will provide key insight about what it feels like to sit in that seat, work with that person, or get your undivided attention.

Cultivating regulars is the job of the manager. Many businesses ask for customers' "valued opinion" as a way to have them buy in to the business and to feel valued. What you really need to do is engage your regulars regarding their experience with your business; they have firsthand experience of your service and all the little things that are under your roof so their opinion can be quite helpful. It is always hard asking for and hearing feedback. But who better to dole it out than someone who is a supporter and a cheerleader and who shows pride in what you do? Use your regulars' feedback to make change in the tactile aspects of what you do, and you can't help but see improvement. The positive relationships you have with a few regulars will be a warming "primer" for the relationship you will develop with your first-time guests. Invite the newcomers to find comfort in your brand, and they can't help but warm up to your business and products as well.

Creature Comforts

The physical aspects of comfort are just as important. Furniture is a wonderful thing and can be a creative representation of your mission and brand. The proper chair is everything, but it isn't easy to pick out a "good" chair. I have worked with chairs that left stains on guests' clothing, that collected more dust than the Museum of Natural History, that are too narrow for most guests to fit in, and chairs that prevent staff from properly serving the guests sitting on those chairs. Chairs can hurt your back, legs, and neck. They can snag your clothing, wobble, and squeak.

Keep in mind that the things your guests come in contact with should enhance their experience of your business. The tactile experiences people have when experiencing your business and items in it will affect their memory of doing business with you. And in this context chairs become a huge challenge. If your chairs leave a stain on a guest's beautiful new suit, are dusty or dirty, are uncomfortable, and then impair the service, you have created at least one unpleasant memory, not just about your customer service, but about the lack of care shown your guest. This is a passive effect as you are not intending to make your guest dirty and uncomfortable, but it is a moment that gets lodged in your guest's mind and now colors the rest of his or her experience.

It is a well-documented phenomenon that when people perceive a positive attribute of a person or thing, they then assume that the person or thing as a whole has other positive traits. This perception colors their experience and creates an "angelic halo" around the person or thing; this is why the psychologist Edward Thorndike named the phenomenon the "halo effect"[6] in 1920. For instance, if someone is attractive, we commonly assume that the person is also smart and kind. Likewise, if the chair we are seated in is comfy and clean, then we assume that the business as a whole is attentive and gracious. This is a common cognitive bias that we all make: when the first impression is good, then the rest of the business has a "halo" of being assumed to be good. In addition, this positive trait and our assumptions about it then become the truth for us; even when other, less positive traits are added later, we hold on to our first impression and take our perception as the truth.

Where you must show caution is with the powerful alter ego of the halo effect called the devil effect. In this case when you experience a negative trait about a person or thing, this negativity now colors your experience. The classic scenario is that when an employee is often tardy for work, others assume the person is lazy and does not care. The trouble is that people don't always look deeper to learn more; they often just take their assumption as truth and go on their merry, oblivious way. The same applies to business: that first impression could be the devil. For example, that uncomfortable chair could indicate that the service will be rushed and impersonal ("I'm uncomfortable; they must not want me here"). The door covered with fingerprints may indicate that the receptionist will be inattentive and dismissive ("If they don't notice all this dirty glass, then they won't pay attention to me"). The worn and old floors may be a sign that the grocery has expired merchandise and not enough stock ("This funky old place is seriously out of date, let's go"). For us as business owners or managers, the devil effect is our worst enemy and forces us to look at everything under our roof.

Let's go back to seating. Like anything else that you are offering to your guests, you must experience all of the customer seating in your business. This means taking time to actually sit in each seat on the premises in quiet times and in busy times. It is important to understand the guest's perspective from each seat in your operation because only then will you have a sense of the experience from that particular vantage point. You must understand what the best seats are and what the worst ones are from a guest's perspective. Is the seat too low to see when the receptionist is calling out to you, or is the reception desk so low that when seated you can see the mess behind the desk? Is the seat near the restroom just another place to sit or is it now the "peek" seat with glimpses at the urinals and sinks every time the door opens? Assess the seats and the relative experience guests have on those seats, and you will learn some amazing facts about your customers' experience.

In my years at Balthazar I took time to experience the seats in the restaurant both as a guest and in my role as maitre d'. There were tables that appeared to be "bad" (near the door, in a busy area, seemingly cramped); however, once seated at the table, it turned out it was a comfortable experience. There were corner tables that by virtue of being in a corner seemed quite posh but were in fact really tight. To assume the corner is going to feel posh to a man who is over 6 feet tall is a mistake; that can only feel cramped to him, and I certainly wouldn't have known this if I hadn't sat there myself in an effort to see and feel the restaurant from the guest's perspective. I was then armed with information: tall men must never be seated at a corner table. And this avoided a situation that might have served up the devil on a silver platter ("If they can't see that I'm over 6 feet, then they must be a bunch of amateurs") and replaces it with a halo of goodness ("They can tell I'm someone special and gave me this nice big table, this place is awesome"). Service can be an angelic or devilish; your focus on the little things helps keep the devils at bay.

Push It or Pull It

The metaphor of doors is powerful. Doors commonly signal a change from one event to the next; in a way, walking through a door is like opening a new chapter. How about that experience when you are trying to push open the door to a business, but it is too heavy to swing open, and you have a computer bag over your shoulder and an umbrella, and perhaps you weren't expecting the door to be quite so heavy? And now you give this "darned door" a second try with a quarterback shove, and the door gives but doesn't quite open? By this time your computer bag is slipping, and now someone else is behind you; that person lends a hand, and with a whoosh, you're inside this business. But what are you left feeling? What are you left remembering? That the door felt like a barrier to your composure and your usual strength, and quite frankly, it was an insult to your ability to do a usually easy task.

The first step toward a sale is now tinged with impressions of folly, of confusion, of frustration. You have just served up "discomfort" on a silver platter, and now everything else has to overcome the effect of this one interaction and its accompanying feelings if a sale is to be made. Clearly, you must make sure that your customers' first interaction with your business is not tinged with a negative impression.

The door of your business really deserves attention, as it is the physical representation of "hello" and "good-bye." The door is one of the first things to impact your customers and one of the last they'll interact with as they leave.

I have seen numerous people upon leaving a business walk with full force into a glass door. Not only is this painful, it leaves your guest feeling embarrassed; as the he tries to regain his composure, his thoughts range from "where did that come from" to "I hope no one saw me"; that is, your guest's thoughts have been directed away from your business. When customers are in your business, you want your brand to remain "front of mind"; physical diversions coming into the customers' awareness, only distract them from your business and your products. You have made it easy for them to "switch the channel" away from your fabulous brand.

Other than the front door, the other most frequently used door in your business is in your bathroom. How many bathrooms have doors that are broken, have jiggly locks, and insecure walls interrupted by cracks so wide that people can see through? People don't want someone to walk in on them in the bathroom where privacy is desired but not always ensured. And how about the lock that no one is really sure is locked? Similarly, in a store the dressing room is an area where people are seeking privacy. In retail stores the dressing room usually is where the sale is made. So when the door doesn't latch, the hooks are broken, and there are dust bunnies in the corner, the message to customers is, "We don't care about your experience in the dressing room, and we don't care about making the sale."

Doors have the power to usher customers into the experience of your business. Some of the most memorable businesses serve to "transport" their customers in very deliberate ways once they step inside the business. For example, Abercrombie and Fitch uses the doors as a border: there, teens cross over into a sensory heaven and any composed adult is barred. Still, even if you don't transport your customers with booming music, half-dressed surfer dudes, and eau de cologne sprayed throughout the sales floor, you do transport them into your world. You create an experience that is professional, unusual, efficient, or helpful and that has your stamp on it. The door becomes the entryway or the barrier to the experience. You want your customers to see your business as a highlight of their day, no matter what you are offering or selling to your guests. It is imperative that the door allows easy access to the upcoming experience and allows your guest to open a new chapter in their day, one entitled "a wonderful customer experience."

No Fear

A client installed a grand marble staircase in the center of her retail space. It was a statement piece and was quite stunning: white marble, gently curving to a graceful landing. Very glamorous to look at but quite perilous to descend. When standing at the top of the stairwell looking down it appeared to be a sheet of ice. There was a handrail on only one side, and the lighting was focused on the artwork on the walls rather than on the steps. After the store had been open a few months, the proprietor, at my suggestion, installed two signs warning people to be careful on the stairs. The lights were made brighter, and black treads were added—all in an attempt to undo the fear that people were feeling traversing this "statement" stairwell.

This is a definite trend; people are focusing on the stairs in their businesses more than ever. I see treads or yellow and black striped tape on the edges of individual steps, all to call attention to potential peril. If not treads, then businesses might install a sign urging customers to use caution when descending the stairs or to hold on to the railing when going up the stairs. Often, stores use signs on the walls and on the individual steps themselves. There are lights focused on the stairs, lights installed on each of the steps, and lights on the top and bottom landing. Often, there is a veritable user manual near stairwells that directs patrons to "please use the handrails and exhibit caution when going down the stairs." Stairs may be inherently dangerous, but they should be a feature that serves to enhance your brand rather than taint it with fear and discomfort.

Here is how to minimize fear or keep it from entering your clients' minds and distracting them from your products and services. You have to take a look around and be vigilant about what is coming in contact with your guests. Go down the stairs, try out the chairs, go into the bathroom, try the lock, try to open the door, try to keep it closed, and make sure there are hooks for your coat and that it all feels sturdy and works correctly. That is the secret: you erase fear when everything works properly and does what it is supposed to do.

Designers may create a space with a beautiful aesthetic and a visual 3-D representation of your brand. But as a business owner you must understand the experience of that design and how it impacts your customers. You must remember that each point of contact from the front door to the pen you offer with a receipt is a means of connecting with your customers physically as well as emotionally. Think about the items that customers will touch and interact with: the doorknob, railing, door, or shopping cart. Each has an impact that is felt by the user, your customer. And each will be retained in the customer's mind as a memory that contributes to (or takes away from) the service experience. The most successful businesses leave no stone unturned to understand how their tactile choices impact each guest; these businesses know that such impressions will last long after the guest has paid and left the building.

Tips and Takeaways

- **A Firsthand Experience**. In the restaurant and hotel business managers are tasked with experiencing the operation regularly; eating in the dining room and sleeping in the rooms. This allows the manager to have a firsthand experience with the most important position in the operation: the guest's point of view. Task your managers to physically interact with the service experience by sitting in the waiting room, walking the showroom floor, and entering the building through the main entrance rather than a back door. This gives them a close-up view of the guests' experience and informs them how to make changes or improvements to the tacit aspects of your business.
- **Feedback Is Essential**. Ask for feedback from your guests about the physical experience of your operation. Inquire about the experience: is it safe, comfortable, clean, and in good working order? Your guests will have plenty of insight on how they experience various aspects of your operation. But don't just ask them, experience it every day to thwart any poor impressions of your space and your stuff.
- **A Watchful Eye**. Many management teams put one person in charge of maintenance of the operation, but it is helpful for everyone to keep a watchful eye on the entire enterprise. Offer programs for the staff that favor and promote cleaning and correcting problems before they start.

Start a logbook for maintenance issues so that everything can be attended to by the right people. Put maintenance issues and fixes in staff newsletters. When staff members see what you are focusing on and that you are willing to make improvements, they understand your core message: we notice, we care, and we act.

- **What Are People Saying?** Look at your Yelp reviews and see if there are any insights into the experience of your physical plant. Are people complaining about a long wait at your music venue because it takes too long or because they are waiting out in the cold? Are they saying they are uncomfortable because of the seating or because of the drafty windows? Read between the lines for more information about the experience of your place, and then improve it, fix it, or change it altogether.

CHAPTER 4

Please Hold

Customer Chagrin

Yvonne and Marco live a challenging life. Although married, they live in different cities due to the nature of their positions at work, and so they must travel hundreds of miles in order to be together every weekend. Each moment counts and they are keen to maximize their precious time together especially when they have the luxury of a long weekend. On one such weekend the couple traveled just outside of Yvonne's home in the south of Germany to visit a new and highly rated spa. Going to a spa together is a common activity for German couples and is culturally considered a great way to connect and relax in a beautiful and restful environment together. The spa they chose is nestled in a charming hilltop town with views of the valley below and mountains in the distance; it's an idyllic spot for a restful day together. It is also a new spa that has already garnered praise for its location, design, and customer service. Yvonne and Marco were primed to be pampered and cared for.

They arrived at the front desk of the spa and noted the beautiful interior: natural elements combining local stone, wood paneling, and floor to ceiling glass walls showing the exquisite view. The very picture of relaxation and retreat. They were set up for a restful experience until the receptionist didn't stop talking on the phone. They waited and smiled. They turned away then turned back awkwardly. They looked toward the view and back at the receptionist, unclear why she still had not put the caller on hold. After about ten minutes she hung up the phone and immediately looked at the computer, then acknowledged them with a hasty, "How can I help you?" No smile, no apology, no warmth at all. This greeting and its preceding wait were not expected and were quite the opposite of a relaxing spa experience. With each passing moment Yvonne and Marco were prevented from starting their spa getaway and were creating a joint memory of displeasure, annoyance, and discomfort.

When they talk about their experience of this new and fabulous spa, the wait at the start of their experience was such an unpromising beginning that everything that followed did not quite make up for it. The two wondered why the receptionist couldn't put the caller on hold or even look at them briefly to acknowledge them. The receptionist's behavior made them feel unconsidered and second-class at a place where they are paying a nice sum for the enjoyment of this beautiful business. And guess what? They will never return, and their word-of-mouth review has now colored the experience for other potential guests.

Problems drive many business transactions. Many products and services are devised in order to take away customers' problems. You're hungry? We have food. You're sick of your old TV? We'll sell you a new one. You're concerned about your future? We have life insurance to help protect your family. You're anxious? I've got a pill for that. This is not just about selling to needy customers but also about identifying the problem and providing a solution. A solution people will pay for. But what invariably happens is that even more problems are created while the customer is with us: businesses routinely ask people to wait, to be patient, and to hold the line while we figure out how to solve their initial issue. It is essential to realize that our business can create discomfort for our guests when additional problems arise, and we must be aware of and address all the additional discomfort we are creating for our customers.

First: what causes discomfort to your clients? If your business has a large number of phone operators, then you can bet there is discomfort while people wait patiently on the phone for customer service. If you sell goods in a retail setting, you must be aware of the checkout process and also of any sort of changing room scenario. If you sell services, you must be aware of your scheduling and appointment times. And then there is often some discomfort that your customer will endure that is partially self-inflicted. I know I am preaching to the choir when I say that most scheduling snafus start with the customer who arrives late or doesn't show up at all, and this throws everything else off.

When I was a maitre d', I could have a perfect night on paper and watch it all fall to pieces as parties arrived late or early or at the wrong time, showed up on the wrong day, or walked in without a reservation. Holding a table for a party that never arrives is a waste of the following customers' time, and it is frustrating to manage. On a given night I routinely had 30 percent of reservations turn out to be no-shows (not arrive and without a call to inform us), or cancellations. As you can imagine, 30 percent is a large number and most of this percentage would be comprised of no-shows, guests who really throw off the timing for all other diners. It is true: scheduling appointments, tables, hotel rooms, and flights are all thwarted by the very people you need to consider: your customers. Sometimes this feels like a lose-lose scenario because you may create a problem for people who have heeded their reservation or appointment time, but you cannot honor it because other guests have not heeded theirs.

This provokes a hustle to fill in the time slot that is now empty or pushed back and this causes discomfort to the unsuspecting and on-time customers. This is a problem that is felt by both the manager and the customers; it produces discomfort from unforeseen circumstances. But as a business owner or manager you must still be on top of it. Blaming the earlier no-shows doesn't offer any resolution to the guests in front of you; you must have a strategy for handling the requisite discomfort you are now asking your guests to endure. In a restaurant the bar is where we keep people while they are waiting, and we can even feed them and give them drinks filled with alcohol to keep them happy. Of course, not every business can have a bar, but the fact is that restaurant owners understand that people have to wait so they had to devise a remedy for this situation. What are the unpleasant situations you ask your guests to endure? What are the problems in your business? What causes discomfort to your valued guests? Whatever it is, you must create "the bar" for them to enjoy themselves while you ask them to endure some discomfort a little longer.

The Psychology of Waiting

Yvonne and Marco are not the only people who dislike waiting; the truth is that no one likes to wait. With many appointment scenarios people have little assurance of their appointment actually being on time, and often the waiting room itself leaves much to be desired. In a seminal article entitled "The Psychology of Waiting Lines"[1] David Maister speaks to the downright agony of waiting, and the impact this has on the customer service experience. There are a number of conditions that impact the customers who are waiting in line for your service; each of these offers an insight that helps to identify the discomfort and find a solution to it. According to Maister the following is true of people waiting:

1. Occupied time feels shorter than unoccupied time.
2. People want to get started.
3. Anxiety makes waits seem longer.
4. Uncertain waits are longer than known, finite waits.
5. Unexplained waits are longer than explained waits.
6. Unfair waits are longer than equitable waits.
7. The more valuable the service, the longer the customer will wait.
8. Solo waits feel longer than group waits.

These are all understandable conditions that help us comprehend what people are going through when they must wait for our service. Each example also highlights the perception of waiting and how uncertainty, in particular, taints the impression customers have of the wait they are experiencing. Perception is reality, so when a customer is in a situation where he or she is perceiving something very different than what is actually happening ("I've been waiting here for hours!"), it will be very hard to convince that person otherwise. It is essential to understand how the points above can impact guests so that you can anticipate and intervene before that perception is created at all.

"Occupied time feels shorter than unoccupied time" is something we can all identify with. According to Maister, people will wait longer when they have something to do; when they are distracted from waiting, they perceive the wait time as shorter. We see this all the time: waiting rooms stocked with the latest magazines, lines at the DMV with TV monitors, and the classic restaurant scenario: the well-stocked bar. These are all strategies to help people forget that they are waiting for their service to begin and to help them fill the time so that "waiting" becomes secondary to "reading," "watching," or "drinking."

Another insight is that people want the service experience to start or get moving. This removes the anxiety people feel while waiting and helps them feel "remembered" or noticed in the service experience. When I was a cocktail waitress in the 1990s, I realized that I would have happier guests when I stopped by my new tables and let them know that I had seen them and would take care of them next rather than rush by. My standard line was "Hello! Please take a look at the menu, and I will be right back to give you my full attention." The promise of service combined with acknowledgment of the customers was key to my success as a waitress because it assured the guests that I had noticed them at the table. By greeting them, I had started their service experience. And who doesn't want someone's full attention? When I promised to return, I promised to give them the full customer service and care that they were seeking. This started the service experience with the greeting (hello), assured the guest that they were seen (I'll be right back), and let them know that the service experience would continue (please look at the menu).

Customers' anxiety is a common condition, according to Maister, and it plays out in many ways. Anxiety is amplified when people are waiting to get started but also when making decisions around their wait. Choosing the express or regular line at the grocery store, pressing the right number when on the customer service phone line, going to the right entrance at the stadium on game day—each decision impacts our wait time. What if we choose wrong? We may have to wait longer, and then it is our own fault. Many supermarkets have several lines that invite people to make a decision: which line will offer the minimum wait? As this is impossible to know the moment of choice is fraught with anxiety and unwittingly pits customers against each other as they stream toward the cashier, some faster, some slower. At the airport the choice between curbside check-in and waiting in line at the counter means choosing between two service lines, and that moment of decision-making increases anxiety about the wait itself.

Once your customer has endured a line it is imperative that the experience following the waiting is flawless. If after waiting patiently for service, customers are met with service that is unfriendly, inefficient, or insensitive to their time, then they will be more perturbed than ever.

One example of this is the evolution of the phone queue for credit card customer service. Long ago, when you called a customer service phone line in any industry, you would get a person who would put you on hold and then come back to you. Over time many companies developed various computerized "queuing systems" in order to maximize the number of customers while also addressing some of the challenges of waiting. Many computerized systems "start the experience" by getting your name, account number, identifying information, and then keeping you "occupied" on the line while playing music or offering a spiel of information about the company or its services.

But the disconnect happened when the real live agent answered the call. She then asked for the same information that the caller obediently had entered when prompted by the computer, which invites the question: "Does the computer system communicate with the operator? Does it even work?" Being asked to share personal information, such as a credit card number, again and again opens up a potential breach in security and safety for that customer's account. Updated versions of the phone queue replace this discomfort of sharing personal information with some discretion. The new system requires the customer to reach out by his or her primary phone number, the number associated with the account. Then all that is required is to enter the last 4 digits of the card number and give a security password that has been chosen by the customer. When the agent comes on the line, she is armed with the account information and only asks for the customer to validate his or her full name. This is efficient customer service that offers real assurance to the customer. It demonstrates that their system has considered the customer by improving the wait time and efficiency of the call and by removing any traces of discomfort associated with calling in the first place.

Innovation in the Magic Kingdom

Of course, the master of the highly designed wait is Disney. Disney practically invented the long, snaking line that held promises of the fun to come, even as the wait was adding up to an hour or more. In fact, Disney was utilizing some of the tenets of Maister's list. The Disney managers give the waiting guests things to do, whether it is watching others pass by in the line, listening to a specialized soundtrack, or seeing photos in real time of other customers on the ride having the time of their life. The Disney people also utilize something they call a "group wait" whereby all the people in the line snake by one another again and again, and this encourages people to interact and connect both about the wait but also about what is coming up next, talking about where the others have been and how it was. These lines have become a standard for most tourist spots, and Disney still uses them daily.

But Disney has also made some changes to the philosophy of "the wait" with its creation of the Fast Pass. This is a kiosk at the beginning of the line that allows customers to print out a ticket with an exact time for them to return. For example, if you arrive at Space Mountain at 11 a.m. with four people in your party, the kiosk will print out a ticket that tells you to return at a later time, perhaps one to two hours later. This allows you to fill in that time with something other than a wait. And it encourages more spending or fun at the park. The wait has been sidelined and filled in with other activities that have meaning for the guests and are also profitable for the business. Ultimately, the wait has turned into a positive and profitable business model for both Disney and the guests.

The second improvement Disney has made is to partner with a tourist company that has an app to download called Lines. It tells users in real time what the wait times are for each ride and thus allows them to plan their day accordingly. There are certain rides that are the main attractions for the park, and these have long wait times most of the day. But there are times when the wait time is shorter, and this allows guests to make smart decisions about their time in the park as a whole. Customers are able to maximize their experience and feel in control of their day; their perception of the experience is improved and the anxiety around the wait has been minimized or eradicated completely.

Now while customers are the first priority in these innovations, it must be said again: the innovations in wait-time management improve the bottom line. At a place like Disney people stay at the park all day. When there are moments between rides and shows, customers will be looking for another distraction and will, in effect, spend more money. This is Disney's "bar." At a restaurant bar customers wait while they "start their experience" by having a drink, which alleviates stress and occupies them. But it is also a way to offer products (both alcoholic and nonalcoholic) that people will purchase and enjoy. Innovation around wait times is a win-win for customers and the business.

Get Them In, Get Them Out

Technology is a great way to update your service. For example, Apple is another customer service giant that uses technology to improve the customer service experience. When shopping at Apple, all you have to do is find an Apple associate and that person can answer your questions but also make the sale without asking you to stand in a cashier line. Apple pioneered the use of iPhones as a point of sale (POS) device, and every associate has the capacity to make a sale for anyone. This helps the customer diminish the dilemma of waiting for service, but it can also inspire a sale as you are on the sales floor among the products. This gives an opportunity for "suggestive selling"; that is, when customers ask for one item, they are also offered any appropriate accessories. You may go to purchase a speaker for your iPod, but you can bet that the sales rep will also take a moment to show you speaker options as well as cases and connectors for your new device. This opportunity is minimized in a traditional retail line, where only some items are offered in the checkout line and there is certainly no associate there to recommend more products.

Many other retail stores are also utilizing mobile POS technology. For example, at Nordstrom Rack and Sephora there is one line for customer checkout and also a number of other salespeople throughout the sales floor who are able to make sales for customers paying by credit card and not in the line. This flexibility can add up to shorter lines in general and less stress for guests who can spot and utilize this expedited service. Having options is alluring for guests who are armed with a credit card and ready to check out. And you must focus on serving these guests as quickly as possible; they are the "express guests," in and out, no questions asked.

The express consumer is one type of customer you want to see increase in your business. Of course, every business will have customers who want a full customer service experience, who will ask questions about products and services, and who will be open to buying more because of the customer service interaction. But your express guests are customers who walk in, ready to make a purchase at any amount, and want to get in and out as quickly as possible, and you must cater to their need of expediency in any way you can. If you can, indeed, get them in and out with what they need in hand, then you can be sure they will return, assured that their time is considered even when they want just a tiny bit of the customer service experience. Your goal is to make sure that even a tiny bit of customer service is memorable for being efficient, swift, and considerate rather than the main event of the buying experience.

When I was a waitress, I loved serving guests I called professional diners. They all fit the profile of the guest who eats out several times a week, usually for business, and who has both a budget for time and a budget for spending. These guests always ordered right away, ordered two to three courses, ordered cocktails and then wine, and did not require too much attention as long as things were flowing smoothly and effortlessly. These diners just wanted things to move along; they wanted to have a nice time with a valued client but didn't want to take all night, and they had a budget to enjoy themselves but didn't need the service to be the entertainment. This was a breeze for me as a server because I could serve and clear and keep the pace going nicely for them. And at the end of the meal everyone was happy: I was able to turn the table for the next party and make more business for the restaurant. And the guests were able to keep to their timetable and budget.

One trend that does not serve these express guests is the number of taps required on a credit card payment pad. We have all experienced the payment moment where we have to tap the pad to indicate credit or debit card, then again to approve the total, then another time to give money to a charitable cause, then again to sign our name, and again to approve the transaction.

These are too many steps and too many things to read and respond to when customers are checking out. Conversely, retailers like Whole Foods and other chains keep the payment moment as short as possible. Once you have swiped your card and approved the total, you have nothing left to do, other than grabbing your receipt and leaving. Many quick-service restaurants (Prêt a Manger, Chipotle, Chop't) do the same, but they accept your card and swipe it without requiring any approvals or signatures. Quick-service restaurants are all about the "throughput" of guests (the time needed to complete one order), and they time the entire experience from ordering to payment. The less time spent in this business, the better for both the guests and the business model: more throughput means more customers can purchase food during the peak hours, and each customer can have more time in his or her day and spend less time waiting in line.

In many luxury businesses there is often a waiting area for both customers and the partners of that customer. This creates a place where the primary consumer can shop and access their most trusted advisor when making decisions about high-ticket items. The secondary consumer in this scenario (the person waiting) is not shopping and so is not occupied; therefore, this guest must have an area where he or she can be occupied while waiting for the moment of conference. These businesses realize that this secondary consumer is key in making the sale. In high-end retail environments the waiting area seating is plush and comfortable; there is usually a table for setting down a bag or displaying some up-to-date, glossy reading material. In many department stores there are a number of cafés dispersed throughout the store so as to provide a break for the shoppers and a distraction for those accompanying them. Cafés, champagne or cocktail bars, yogurt bars, and coffee stands are all common in many stores and shops. In upscale offices the waiting area is often equipped with mineral water, a selection of hot beverages, and even candy or snacks.

A Beautiful Distraction

Elevators are not an entirely modern convenience. There is evidence that early elevators were in use in mines in the third century CE. They were powered by humans, animals, or waterwheels and were an impressive innovation. King Louis XV of France famously had an elevator installed in Versailles in 1743 for the purpose of reaching his mistress who was installed in a room one floor above his. It was man-powered and utilized a counterweight but was still somewhat primitive as it was not equipped with a brake. Despite this safety flaw, at the time it was considered a cutting-edge convenience, fit for a king.

Elevators as we know them now were engineered in the mid 1800s. Powered by steam and equipped with a hand brake, they made it possible to build skyscrapers, and they were the precursors of the elevators of today. When first invented, all elevators were a great convenience and a huge asset in any building. But even when convenient, elevators soon became a point of discomfort for passengers as they were deemed too slow and were a place of anxiety and distress.

One hotel received a number of complaints about the long wait times for the elevators in the lobby. The hotel researched the equipment, and there was not much improvement to be made. The hotel manager then thought that perhaps if the guests were distracted from waiting, they might not perceive the wait as long and—voilà!—the hotel installed mirrors around the elevator bank. This was the magic distraction; it allowed the customers a beautiful reflection of themselves and the environment, which kept them from counting the minutes while waiting for the elevator to arrive. The complaints stopped, and the hotel had started a trend: improving elevator experiences for customers. This urban legend has spurred many innovations in elevator comfort we experience today.

This is at the heart of avoiding discomfort: distraction. When you knowingly create distractions for your guests, you are filling time and creating comfort. Comfortable guests will trust you because they have the feeling that their experience is moving along and that they are being considered. You must assume your clients, customers, and guests are coming to you with some sort of problem to solve. When I was a maitre d', I always had to remind myself that people arrive at a restaurant hungry. And I know that when I am hungry, I get short-tempered, cranky, impatient, and weary. Understanding that most of my guests would be arriving feeling hungry and all the accompanying uncomfortable feelings, empowered me to solve their problems by distracting them from their problem: hunger. I always say "In a restaurant we have so much with which to make people happy." So instead of adding more discomfort, I worked on addressing customers' immediate pain and occupied my guests and sometimes even sent them a little something to nibble on.

People are complicated creatures, but they are your guests and patrons so you must do your best to understand them, especially when there is a wait or a bit of discomfort to be endured. Your job is not to rip off the band-aid and create more pain; your job is to soothe, distract, and impact through a positive and meaningful customer service experience.

Tips and Takeaways

- **Time It**. Pay attention to the wait times of your guests at the cash register, as they enter, when they are on the phone or online with your business. Depending on your type of business, you may have just seconds of your customers' goodwill before you will start to lose them to the dismay of waiting. Work with your team to create efficiencies around common wait times and give your team resources for keeping your clients engaged positively when they have had to wait for a very long time. And always remember to thank customers for their patience when you are able to give them your full attention. A sincere acknowledgment will go a long way in this service recovery moment.

- **Use Customer Surveys**. Conduct an e-mail survey for your guests to fill out about the wait in the store or on the phone. You can get a sense of how challenged your guests feel by any sort of wait at your operation. Or don't wait that long; For example, Athleta is a sports apparel retailer that has a dedicated customer feedback computer set up in its retail stores. The company invites customers to answer the survey questions, and by doing they are entered to win a possible shopping spree. This is a great incentive for customers to respond to a survey and helps to capture the moment while they are in the store.

- **Create Distractions.** What are some ways you can create distractions for your guests as they are waiting in your business? Having magazines on hand or a TV are classic distractions, but perhaps there are other ways to engage your customers that focus on your brand and represent your culture or ethos? Display books that represent your commitment to the environment, core values, or connection to a specific charity or sporting event. Use your distractions to promote your brand and tell a story about your company.

- **Invite Staff Insight.** Your staff is on the front lines of service. Staff members are aware of the inefficiencies that are a barrier to swift service. Engage with your staff to gain insights about impediments to service that add to wait times. Sometimes the small improvements can have a major impact on the customer service experience. Involve your staff in these improvements and share the timelines for improvement that will affect the various waiting areas of your business. By doing so you show staff members that you value their input and that they make a difference to the customer service experience.

CHAPTER 5

Say What?

Good Manners Count

Adam Weiner is in staff placement. A former lawyer and a chef, Adam combines his professional skills as an instructor at a vocational school called Job Train, and a key part of his job is to place his graduates with various restaurants and hotels in the Silicon Valley area. One of the things he notices about many restaurant and hotel kitchens is that the notion of phone manners has been entirely abandoned. His phone horror stories range from awful to absurd. One call to a colleague at a high-end hotel was answered with "What!?" and he was directed to "call back later, the chef is busy!" Another call he made in response to an SOS e-mail from a recruiter went straight to voicemail and was not answered—that day or the next. And in one extreme lapse one call to a restaurant was answered, but when Weiner asked for the chef, the person who answered the call merely put the phone down on the desk and walked away without a word. Chef Weiner, assuming the staff member was going to get his boss was left to wait. After ten minutes he hung up and redialed, only to get a busy signal.

Unfortunately, scenarios like this are all-too common in any type of business. How people answer the phone speaks volumes about the business being called. Chef Weiner recounts that when he connects with the people who are in need of staff, they are often upset that he had not responded earlier to their call or e-mail. The unnecessary stress and miscommunication due to the lack of guidelines for doing a basic task—answering the phone—has become a major point of discomfort for customers.

Answering the phone is a key moment of service as it greets and sets the tone for the experience the caller will have. The language the staff member uses is critical in setting up the success of this experience. "What!?" is simply not acceptable, ever. But if you have not trained your team or given them proper notes on etiquette, then they simply won't know what is expected of them. Most people on your staff have grown up exting, and phone etiquette has gone by the wayside. Etiquette is not innate; it is learned, so you must train your team in etiquette and the proper language to use. On the phone all there is is language; there are no other distractions. Many "service scripts" are devised for the phone aspect of the customer experience because the phone has so many limitations.

Because on the phone you are limited to words, you must make sure you are giving the people on your team good verbal options for each moment of service on the phone and teach them the appropriate tone in which to convey the words. Common moments include the greeting, putting someone on hold, answering questions, and handling complaints. For my clients I even create a standard operating procedure for handling customer feedback and compliments. This might seem easy, but your staff members must exude graciousness and your business must provide a protocol for every type of guest interaction and feedback your staff members may encounter.

Putting someone on hold is tricky; no one likes to be made to wait, and it adds discomfort to this customer experience. In service scripts that I write for the phone I always write a piece on "putting someone on hold" that goes like this:

- If you need to put the guest on hold, ask first, and wait for a response. "May I put you on hold for a moment, please?" When the person says "yes," respond with "thank you!"
- After returning to the line, say "Thank you so much for holding; how may I help you?"
- If the first call is taking more time than you expected (running more than 30 seconds), please return to the holding caller and ask if the person

might like for you to ring back at the conclusion of your other call. "I'm so sorry, this call is taking more time than expected. May I take your name and number and ring you back?" When the caller responds in the affirmative, say "Thank you so much, [insert caller's name], I will call you in about 2 minutes."

My goal in writing this out is to capture the tone of the business, the etiquette (using "please" and "thank you") and a time frame. This lets the staff member know in detail how to take phone calls. The 30-second mark is important as it tells callers that you value their time and are keeping your promise when quoting a time. If you keep this small promise ("I'll call you back in 2 minutes"), you bring trust to the guests' experience.

When creating a phone service script or guideline, you may want to add little tricks for adding more personality to the phone experience. Smiling when speaking makes an audible difference. When people smile as they are speaking on the phone, the person on the other end can "hear" the smile in the voice, and this adds warmth and humanity to the call. Another trick is to have a mirror positioned in a convenient place in your office or cubicle so that you can observe yourself when you are engaging with a customer on a phone call.

For example, Veronica Jenkins is the operations manager at a large telecommunications company, and years ago she discovered this trick after her boyfriend commented that he could hear her smiling when they were on the phone. Each time she smiled he said she sounded "happier," and he would always ask "are you smiling now?" and she was. She wanted her team to sound "happier" on the phone as well, so she now shares this trick of looking into a mirror in the company training seminars she conducts and in one-on-one mentoring sessions. She knows that this gives immediate feedback to the phone operators or receptionists because they can see their own reactions in the mirror and then correct or respond to what they see.

While smiling helps project happiness, the mirror technique can also help when projecting other, more serious emotions. When a caller has a complaint, the receptionist can see in the mirror whether he or she is reacting appropriately to this call. Concern is made visible in a furrowed brow, a downturned smile, and a tilt of the head; all these are authentic reactions that come from compassion. Just say "oh, no! I'm so sorry to hear it!" out loud, and you will feel your face naturally project sorrow and concern. Facial movements express authentic human feelings, and this can have a powerful impact when on a phone call and can turn a remote experience into one filled with authentic emotion and compassion.

A Little Respect

Language is the way you demonstrate appreciation and respect for your guests. You must always remind yourself that you are often speaking with strangers, and for this reason alone you must offer some caution and respect for everyone you are engaging with. One way to show an increased (but not overdone) formality is to speak in full sentences or avoid single word responses. For example, "What's up?" gets replaced with "How may I help you today?" And "Over there" gets replaced with "You can find that item on the left side of aisle 12," and "Next" gets replaced with "May I help the next guest?" This small adjustment can make a customer feel like a valued guest. The complete sentence conveys a bit of attention that is lacking from the single word response, which seems abrupt or curt. A sentence demonstrates engagement and starts a conversation, one in which the guest also has a say and a role.

Etiquette is a formalized way of showing respect. Manners demonstrate respect for the person in front of us. By using Mr. or Ms. with someone's name you are telling that person that you do not assume a level of friendship or familiarity and that you are taking a professional approach. Etiquette is a social construct and still has a place in our world. While "sir" and "madam" may have lost ground in some arenas, the formality people crave is one that demonstrates that they are in a valued position. Customers should always be made aware that they are the guests, that they are valued clients and the very reason why you are in business in the first place. Your customers are the ones you are working for, and their satisfaction is your goal. Lest you forget, the power is in the hands of the consumers; a common phrase to describe this power is "vote with your wallet." And because this is true, you must demonstrate through every little thing you do that you are putting your customers first.

The Predictive Group conducts studies that utilize the Predictive Index, an instrument that helps to determine personality behaviors and how they trend with predictable traits associated with job performance. Highlights from a study the group conducted entitled "The Predictive Index Customer Service Rep (CSR) Study"[1] (published on their website) proved that formality in call center service representatives was highly valued. The reps who performed better were seen as having higher formality and lower extroversion than the group that performed less well. In the survey, formality was demonstrated with "a manner that is careful, precise, accurate and detail-oriented." Lower extroversion was demonstrated as "a communication style that is character- ized by politeness, sincerity, respectfulness, and a sense of propriety, with a strong desire to say and do the right thing in the best interest of the cus- tomer." The group that performed less well showed traits of extroversion that demonstrated free-form speech rather than following the script; people in that group talked more with their coworkers and acted more "chatty" with their clients. This lack of formality was equated to worse customer service and reduced client satisfaction by 20 percent in the study.

In the study of linguistics formality is a specific way of speaking. The *Longman Dictionary of Language Teaching and Applied Linguistics*[2] defines formality in language as "the type of speech used in situations when the speaker is very careful about pronunciation and choice of words and sen- tence structure." In a paper on linguistics entitled "Formality of Language: Definition and Measurement"[3] the authors, Francis Heylighen and Jean- Marc Dewaele, classify formality in language as "an attempt to avoid ambi- guity." When people are using informal speech, they rely on context (about a place, person, or thing), use more "unstated assumptions" (ideas that seem obvious), and are more casual in their verbal choices.

One of the examples mentioned in the article of informal as opposed to formal speech is the informal "I'll see him tomorrow." This can be rephrased more formally as "Karen Jones will see John Smith on October 13, 2015." "I'll see him tomorrow" demonstrates the context of knowing the day and makes the unstated assumption that the listener knows who "him" is. More formal speech removes the doubt by filling in the blanks of date and the names of the people involved. In the Predictive Group study, this sort of formality was valued in the customer service interactions because the formal style of language removed doubt in the mind of the callers.

In 2008 I was retained by the New Jersey Performing Arts Center to improve the service at its pre-theater fine dining restaurant. The staff was mostly new to the restaurant business, and the service had been suffering for quite some time. The first day I was on site, I was introduced to the CEO. He had only one thing to say to me: "Please make them stop saying 'no problem,' I hate that!" When I asked why he had such a strong reaction, his answer was short and sweet: "is there a problem I should know about? If not, don't put this idea in any customer's mind." Well said. As I worked with the team this became my mission: to erase a common colloquialism from the staff's vocabulary at this high-volume restaurant.

Why do people use the phrase "no problem" in the first place? People commonly use it in place of other phrases: "You're welcome," "Of course," and "Right away." The problem with "no problem" is that it replaces something slightly more formal. Many people have a strong reaction to this phrase and other casual responses. Hearing "yeah" instead of "yes," "what" instead of "excuse me," and in restaurants "are you still working on that" rather than "may I clear your plate" are all common complaints from guests in customer service situations. As casual as society has gotten in terms of manners and conversation, most people still want to see signs of respect when they are customers. And your job is to demonstrate that respect through the language you choose.

The ABCs

I always say "service is a conversation." It is not a monologue, a soliloquy, or a lecture. People don't want to be talked "at," they want to be spoken "with" and are more receptive when a staff member demonstrates care through the language he or she chooses. People often become annoyed when a salesperson launches into a pitch about a product or service without finding out what the customer is looking for in the first place. There is no such thing as a customer service mind reader; you must engage your guests by conversing with them and then tell them what *they want* to know more about. You also must "read the guest" and feel out what is interesting to her or him before you plunge in with information that may not be relevant. If you work at Abercrombie and Fitch and you approach a man who looks to be in his sixties or seventies and ask if he needs help, you should not assume that he is there buying for his grandkids; he may be there to buy a sweater for himself or a T-shirt for his wife. Engage the person in conversation and find out who your guest is buying for and what he is seeking. Then you can tailor the conversation to what might invite him to buy and leave happy. And the way to do this is through the use of respectful and thoughtful language choices.

You must train your team in the language you want them to use when speaking to guests. For example, when your employees all use the same key words in their interactions with the public, they are reinforcing your brand by "speaking the same language." When you create a common language, this reaffirms and defines your company's culture. "Hello" is the perfect starting place. If you own a surf-inspired store, you may want to impart a feeling of beach culture, a "hang ten" mentality and an ocean-focused lifestyle. You may choose to use words that pull from the surfing culture, and you may ask your staff to greet guests with "Mahalo" (Hawaiian for "hello") or a more casual "hey, welcome to the surf shop!" The point is that the language should support the brand image and philosophy.

To stay with the surf shop example, you may want to coin some signature words for common areas in your operation. You may name the changing rooms "changing huts," the cash register the "deck" (the top of the board), and call your staff members "Mavericks" (after the legendary surfing spot in California). It doesn't have to be goofy, but it can be fun and inclusive for your team members and lend an air of authenticity for those who are listening in. These words and phrases create a bond between team members and become a verbal piece of your brand that gets shared among your clients as well.

Written language is also very important. How you express yourself and represent your business on the Internet, on paper, and on your awning are all choices that determine how your business is perceived by your customers. There are books and websites devoted to the misspellings and misuse of language in many types of businesses. The classics are foreign-language misspellings and the feeling these elicit is "English is clearly a second language, they simply don't know any better." Which is a pretty tame response. But what if your brochure has a misspelling, and you are now regarded as careless, thoughtless, negligent, or sloppy? These are all controllable impressions that generate unfavorable emotions, so you must read, edit, and choose well. Deciding it is not a big deal can actually be a deal breaker for your guests.

At Per Se, a restaurant renowned for its world-class food and impeccable service, the menu was created daily and utilized many different cooking techniques and various foods from all over the world. Part of our task as managers was to proofread the menu before every service. It took five people to ensure that the menu was proper in every way. But this menu with its particular verbiage, multiple languages, and singular style was a defining piece of the restaurant. The care we took with the menu was apparent to everyone who read and ordered from it. And that was exactly the point. Now does every business have to show the same care and diligence? Yes, of course. But it has to match what you are trying to accomplish, and you must utilize the language that supports your vision. Misspellings on a menu or incorrect references on a website—these are all too common, and offer the potential guest a reason to doubt your business. No business wants to be doubted before the transaction has even occurred. Your use of language will define you: talk about it with your staff and proofread all of your materials.

Your logo or a signature product or service represents your business, but your brand is constantly reinforced by your language choices. You have to create a language of common sense by talking through every moment of the customer service experience with your staff. You must choose language that reaffirms your culture by selecting words that are culture-centric and banishing words that are not. The greeting is essential and can be repeated at various moments and with different team members throughout the guests' experience. You must now identify what the next moments of customer contact are and create language that is appropriate to it. In print, online, and in person, language makes your brand more memorable, word by word.

No Ego

In conversing with a client you must remember that your language needs to be "client-focused." You must choose words that will draw people in, that will focus on them and not on you. Good customer service is not business-centered or staff-centered. There must be as little ego as possible in the language you use in your business. Even though the language is all about representing your brand, it must be customer inclusive. For instance, when I am training employees in a restaurant, I banish the word "I" and replace it with "we," "our," or "our customers." When speaking about a product rather than saying "I love the rib eye steak," I recommend that employees say "The rib eye is one of our most popular entrees." This highlights the product without being ego-focused and lets the customer choose something because of the merits of that product itself. This is important because if you tell me you love it, but I don't want it, I may disappoint you in some way. My feelings may have just impacted our relationship. And the stakes get higher when I actually take your advice: if I take your advice and then I don't like the item, there is now a divide between you and me. This just made a simple action (ordering a steak) a personal choice colored by risky personal attachment.

It is your job to help your teams talk about your products. You must arm them with options to use in order to help them be comfortable and easily speak about the products and services you sell. One default selling technique is to pit one item against another: "That one is good, but *this* one is great!" But by doing so you have just damaged your brand. Why would you make, feature, or carry an inferior product to begin with? If you use comparisons to help us sell, you must be very careful. Take online shopping. Customers are often given a way to "compare" certain items based on their features. When buying a laptop, one can compare the processor, memory, display, camera, inputs, and price. And in comparing these items customers are making a choice based on these features and what the features mean to them. Making choices is entirely personal so when being asked to "compare" items in person, our staff members must highlight the differences in the product so that our customers can make the best decision possible. And then they must help the customer focus on what he or she wants in this particular moment. It is easy to tell a customer "I think you should buy this, I love it." But you must remember that you are in the business of customer satisfaction and must keep the focus on your customers, their happiness, and their experience.

It is important to give your staff options for how to handle frequent customer interactions. One thing I always develop for my clients is a fact sheet or a list of FAQs. It contains the basic information all employees should know (the address, phone number, names of the owners, etc.) but can extend to other areas as well (answers about artwork, design details, or a photo gallery of VIPs). What are the frequently asked questions in your business? Often the fact sheet includes answers to questions about what's in the area (nearby ATMs, drugstores, or hotels), directions (travel by car, rail, bus, and parking), various procedures (getting through security, payment options, and reservations), or even safety (where to find the nearest hospital or police station).

What is equally important is not only answering *what* but giving examples of *how*. You must devise appropriate answers that feature a branded, conversational response. Then when someone calls and asks for the address, the proper answer is: "We are located at the corner of 38th Street and Park Avenue, on the northeast corner; you'll enter under the brown awning," which gives more information than "212 East 38th Street." While the second answer is correct, the more detailed and formal first example is the one that puts the guest front and center. You have to give examples of how to handle basic questions so that the information is concise and consistent and makes sense for new customers.

Holy Cow!

Not too long ago, I had an appointment to see one of my favorite doctors. I arrived and took a seat, but while I was waiting a storm was a brewing at the reception desk. On this day it seemed that one of the employees was new. The phone was ringing nonstop, and this new receptionist was one of two people behind the desk; it was clear that the job was getting the best of him. The phone was ringing steadily, and as he finished one phone call, the phone immediately rang again; he sighed audibly and answered the call.

He seemed to have problems communicating with the person on the other end and had to repeat his questions a couple times: "What time would you like...no, what time is good for you? Yes, what time is best?" It sounded frustrating. He completed the call graciously and hung up only to have the phone immediately ring again. "Jesus Christ!" he exclaimed before answering the call.

I was one of two people waiting, and he certainly got my attention. He was showing little discretion at this point and had no sense that the waiting patients heard his colorful words. He completed this call, and the phone rang again. At this point a coworker was also showing him another task that he had to complete, and he muttered to her "these phones just won't stop!" He was clearly frazzled and picked up the line. Another call came in, and he let out a slow and loud "HO-ly CHRIS-tmas!" and answered the phone. This guy was swamped, and no one was helping, addressing his discomfort, or making him aware that every word he uttered was being projected into the waiting area. We were both becoming more uncomfortable and doubtful that this part of the operation was working as smoothly as it should.

Customers will hear your employees on the phone, they will observe them outside of your business, and some staff members will actually go to the homes of your customers. Therefore, it is vital to ensure that the language they use while on the clock represents your business properly and professionally. In a mall setting everyone eats at the food court, both patrons of the stores and the people who work there. So if your staff members are on the clock, are wearing the team uniform, and are on break, they must be made aware that they are still representing the brand, both in their actions and on their shirts. Profane language, inappropriate behavior, and off-color stories may represent them specifically, but they also reflect on your business secondarily. Language guidelines must be established for every moment that staff members are on the clock or on your property. And how staff members handle themselves in public while representing your brand is key because it can deepen the faith customers have in your business or create doubt. Imagine if you were a customer who had just purchased something. You're feeling good about your purchase and then as you are departing the store you overhear a staff member talking on his cell phone complaining about how stupid his boss is. Of course, this colors your experience as a customer. Customers in such a situation will remember that the staff member said the boss was stupid, and they will think one of two things. Either "I bet the boss IS stupid," or "Wow, that guy is disrespectful, I wonder what's going on in there?" Obviously, having guidelines for employees regarding their proper use of language is essential, on and off the business premises.

Language is one of the important messengers of service. How you and your staff communicate with your guests is key as it represents you, your vision, your culture, and your goals. The words that you choose to use for your business are important: the words on the brochure, website, signage, and in your outgoing phone message all contribute to the impression your guests have of your business. Language is so basic that it is often overlooked; listen to your staff members: do they represent themselves as a part of your brand? You must ensure that they do, as each interaction your employees have with your guests, and the language they utilize, will leave a strong impression on your customers.

Tips and Takeaways

- **Follow the Rules**. As the boss, manager, or leader you have to demonstrate the company culture and represent the brand at all times. Just as in parenting, you cannot set up the rules only to break them. If your company culture is known for its playful or humorous side, you must ensure that the humor doesn't break the rules as well. Humor that utilizes language that can denigrate the brand or any person who works for the brand is doing your business a disservice. Funny impressions that make fun of cultural language pronunciations, clever as they may appear, may be doing damage by disrespecting someone's native language. Language is a loud messenger and can misrepresent your authority and, in turn, cause the team to lose respect.
- **Create Common Denominators**. Ask your staff members if there are any questions that they hear more often than others. If so, it may be that

the descriptions your business uses on the website or in written materials are not descriptive enough. Ask your team where the quandaries lie, what the issues are, and what customers seem to be confused about. Then look at the areas in question and revisit and edit your materials, signage, or service scripts to enhance customers' comprehension of your brand and offerings.

- **Play with It**. Think about your core values and how to express your essential philosophy to your team: is it earnest, serious, playful, or conscientious? Play with different approaches to your core values and their wording so that the essence of your business is revealed. For example, I constructed core values for one client by interviewing the team to discover "what mattered" about their service. The director of operations said he wanted his team to "be a chameleon," that is, be part of a breed that can change and adjust with the situation you are in. This became the first core value and sets the tone for the staff members when they come on board.

- **Connect with Others to See the Light**. Every author needs an editor and all written language needs to be checked by another set of eyes to ensure the words are doing their job. Have someone in your business check your materials and written language for proper grammar, repetitious ideas or words, and outdated information. Involve your team members in keeping the written materials that the guests see—and the staff uses—fresh and updated by editing them regularly.

CHAPTER 6

There Is No Such Thing as Medium Rare

Satisfaction

Cassie is a young entrepreneur who loves fashion. When she needs to improve her wardrobe she picks and chooses where to spend her hard-earned cash, and one place she can always count on for a great pair of jeans is the upscale department store Barney's. Cassie loves this store not only for its amazing selection of up-to-the-minute fashions but also for the amazing staff. When she needs a new pair of jeans, all Cassie has to do is go to the denim section, tell the clerk the fit she likes and her size, and they will select four or five pairs and set her up in a fitting room. The beauty of this is that the sales-people (both men and women) are so knowledgeable about their products that Cassie always walks out with one or two perfect pairs of jeans.

One day in September, Cassie went to the store and as usual, walked out with two pairs of jeans. One was more casual with some distress marks and a lighter color, and the other was more classic: perfect, unmarked denim with minimal stitching and design. As the months went by Cassie noticed that one pair of jeans was starting to fray along the inseam; it was not the more casual style but the more traditional pair. She wore each pair only a few times a month, washed them in cold water, and hung them up to dry. Why was one fraying and the other not? In January the fraying jeans completely opened up along the seam, a hole of about two inches had opened, and Cassie shared her disappointment with a friend; she was not sure what to do. "Bring them back to Barney's," said her sage advisor. Cassie heeded the recommendation despite being worried that four months had passed and she had worn the jeans a number of times.

Up at Barney's, the salespeople took one look at the hole and asked if she would like a refund or another pair of jeans. When she asked for another pair like the other pair she had bought, the salesperson went and got her the replacement pair in her size and rang her up in under 10 minutes. Cassie was relieved and thankful that her purchase was so easily returned but also that the clerk never questioned her about the pants or the time it took to return them. Now she often repeats this story, especially when she hears anyone complaining about bad customer service, and it enhances her already glowing reviews of the shopping experience at Barney's.

This is a classic story about customer satisfaction. In order to satisfy a loyal customer, the salesperson needed to make some decisions that satisfied Cassie on the spot. The error was in the product, and the customer was made to feel valued rather than responsible for the damage. No one wants to be considered a "complainer," and when something is not to your customers' liking or does not meet their expectation, you must try to act on behalf of your guests and correct the situation. Even when this sometimes goes against your own perception of what is "correct" or "perfect."

I always tell my culinary students that they must come to grips with the fact that there is no such thing as medium rare, to their shock and dismay. In cooking school the epitome of success is being able to cook all proteins medium rare and know that medium rare has been achieved not by the temperature of the steak but by touching it and knowing what a medium rare steak feels like. Debunking this skill as irrelevant seems like a low blow. What I am trying to impart is that no matter how "perfect" your medium rare might be, there will always be someone who wanted the meat more rare and someone who wanted it more cooked. It doesn't really matter if the steak is cooked perfectly; if the customer is not happy, he or she will not become a return guest. Thus, in the end it is about satisfaction, not perfection. As a service representative, your job is not to defend your position or "school" the customer even if he or she is mistaken. Instead, you should aim to understand what would satisfy the customer in that moment. Satisfaction for the guest will reap great rewards again and again.

Anticipation

Nothing feels better than a natural high. Dopamine is a chemical produced in our bodies that gets released when something good happens; it elicits feelings of pleasure, excitement, and satisfaction by activating our brain's reward center. When we are experiencing pleasurable or positive experiences, dopamine tells us that we are being rewarded, and this leads to the feeling of satisfaction. But dopamine is more closely linked to "seeking" rather than to "liking" responses.

Shopping is a major dopamine stimulant because shopping is a seeking state. This explains the fun of window-shopping and browsing through sales racks, and it also tells us that "shopping" is more important than "buying." In the *Wall Street Journal* article "This is Your Brain at the Mall: Why Shopping Makes you Feel So Good," Tara Parker-Pope explains that in various studies, MRIs (magnetic resonance imaging) of the brain indicate that shopping and dopamine are closely linked. The main dopamine surge occurs in anticipation of a purchase rather than in the experience of the purchase itself. This is good information for anyone selling goods or services: the dopamine surge that signals satisfaction is happening before the customer even experiences the product. Thus, the most important (and pleasurable) moments are those leading up to a sale. Once the sale is complete, the dopamine subsides, leaving the feeling of satisfaction intact.

Your job is to ensure that the buying experience is satisfactory in order for your guests to feel truly "chemically" satisfied. You want your customers to feel the flood of goodness, excitement, and pleasure as they are experiencing your brand and want them to ride that dopamine wave as long as possible. You must remember that shopping is actually more important than the buying; this is the experience that truly counts in the mind of the consumer.

But dopamine can also lead to bad purchasing decisions. Customers get wrapped up in the shopping experience and focus on the wonderful feelings they have about that jacket (that never gets worn), that juicer (that collects dust in the closet), or the collectible figurine that is part of a rare set from 1945 (that sits in the box stashed under the bed). They get caught up in the moment as it is filled with good feelings of anticipation, pleasure, and the success of scoring a bargain, and yet end up with a credit card bill and a house full of unused things. "Buyer's remorse" is the flip side of the dopamine-fueled shopping experience. Once they have taken their purchase home, customers often realize that they will never wear the jacket, don't need the juicer, and can't afford the collectible figurine. This accounts for the impressive return policies in place at many large retailers. Many stores and websites offer "no questions asked" return policies for 30 or even 90 days. They know that buyer's remorse is real and that the ability to return an unused item will keep that customer happy and satisfied even in lieu of a sale.

Managing Expectations

The feeling of satisfaction is not only about getting what you paid for, it is about getting what you want. This is why the medium rare steak example is so important. It doesn't matter if you eat the entire steak; what matters is that what you want (that medium rare bite) is delivered as you expect it. How we, as customers, picture and enunciate our expectation varies greatly. Just trying to describe and find the right color for your home or the right haircut for your personal style is fraught with challenge: expressing the picture in your mind is very hard.

Just ask Susan. When she and her husband decided to renovate their kitchen, they spent time with their contractor and various subcontractors trying to express their vision. Sometimes they felt they expressed their vision accurately, and other times something got lost in translation. "I thought I might have been unclear when I was telling the cabinetmaker how we wanted the finish to look," Susan said. "I think he had a different idea of the end result." She was expecting, and picturing, a rich dark stain on her cabinets that revealed the grain of the wood below, something clearly wooden and rich with color. On the day of the work the owner of the refinishing company had some doubt: the work was progressing as he had instructed his team, but he had a nagging feeling it might not be what his client wanted. Halfway through the process, he checked in on the progress of the cabinets and saw that the color was quite opaque and covered up the wood grain of the cabinets. With a sense of urgency he ran and got Susan to see if what they were doing was to her liking. Turns out, it was not.

He grabbed a cabinet door and wiped a towel across the surface, removing some of the stain. "Is this what you're thinking?" he asked. Susan sighed with relief; indeed it was. In that moment the cabinetmaker mobilized the entire team to wipe down the stained cabinet fronts to reveal the perfect color saturation. A crisis was averted, and satisfaction was assured. The cabinetmaker's action was the key to solving what could have turned a customer complaint into complete customer dissatisfaction.

Human Nature

Expectations are very hard to meet. When I was at Per Se, we were voted #7 on the San Pellegrino list of top 100 restaurants in the world. The number 7 restaurant in the world! The pressure we felt once this was awarded was huge. This meant that now our guests' expectations were going to be even higher, and meeting their varied and exceptionally high expectations was a daily task. Even with accolades and awards we could not relax our standards even for one day or assume that yesterday's experience would carry over to today's reality. The lesson here is to always do what you do as well as you possibly can, every day and with every guest. This is an exercise in excellence: if you strive to meet your own high standards, you will surely meet your customers' expectations along the way.

Every business will set up an expectation for its customers that will tell them what they can anticipate. The expectation is set in many different ways: through branding and web presence, through customer reviews and word of mouth, and most important, through the actual guest experience. Your guests will arrive looking forward to the experience you have told them to expect. When the experience doesn't match the expectation, then this is where dissatisfaction begins. The equation:

Expectations − Performance = (Dis)Satisfaction

is abundantly true.

One night, a trio of colleagues discovered this equation for themselves when they decided to visit a highly rated Italian restaurant for a late dinner.

They arrived at the restaurant around 10 p.m., hungry and happy to share a meal after a long, productive day. The restaurant was busy, but at 10 p.m. the colleagues were hoping to get a table. They arrived at the front desk and asked for a table for three. The host, without looking at her book, immediately told them the wait would be "about 45 minutes to an hour." Carlos took the lead and inquired if there might be something sooner than that to which she replied, "you can eat something at the bar" while gesturing in the general direction of the long bar. The three, somewhat surprised that there was such a wait when there weren't many people there waiting, sidled down the bar where there were two empty seats. Before they could sit down another host rushed at them from behind. She exclaimed, "Those seats are reserved! You can't sit there!" She was pointing at the seats, and her tone was exasperated and irritated.

The trio backed off, apologized, and said that they had been sent to the bar by the other host. At this time there were now two barriers to having dinner, the wait for the table and the host telling them to leave the bar seats. They reluctantly gave it one more shot as the first host found them two other seats at the front of the bar by the front door. They took off their jackets, and the bartender brought drink menus and a food menu. But the trio couldn't relax and didn't feel welcome from all the commotion that had just occurred. In fact, the three colleagues were irritated as well; they were hungry and while they had previously been in a good mood, that good mood was swiftly being erased by every interaction with the restaurant staff. They conferred and decided to leave. As they put on their jackets, the bartender swooped in and asked, "Is everything all right? Can I get you a drink?" But this was too little, too late, and the group left the restaurant hastily to seek dinner elsewhere.

There is a well-documented human response known as the fight-or-flight response.[1] When we are undergoing experiences of extreme stress—when we believe we are in danger—our bodies are conditioned to respond by fighting or fleeing the situation. Many things can inspire this response: trauma, fear, perceived threat, or imminent danger can bring on the response with a rush of hormones to push us into action. Epinephrine starts to surge through the body in response to the incoming danger message in order to fuel our decision to fight or flee, and this hormonal surge gives us the stamina and guts to do what it takes in this moment of stress. It is the "ammunition" our bodies need to fight the threat before us.

The feeling of dissatisfaction has been found to inspire the fight-or-flight response as well. Thus, imagine when your customer is not getting what she asked for or is forced to return a faulty item and is starting to feel the beginnings of dissatisfaction with your products or services. The expectation and performance are not in alignment, and the beginnings of dissatisfaction are starting to rumble in your customer's brain. The customer may display annoyance or agitation and may be in the beginning stages of a flight-or-fight response brought on by dissatisfaction with your brand. When people seem unreasonable it is not merely that they are dissatisfied with you; they are responding to their situation through a haze of hormone-distorted emotions. The hormonal rush of epinephrine may be setting off a basic response to fight with you or make the whole thing go away by leaving. This is not a response you want your customer to get caught up in; the customer will lose his or her reason before you can make any adjustments or improvements to the particular situation.

A component of satisfaction is gratification. Gratification is a feeling of pleasure or happiness when achieving satisfaction or a goal and achieving gratification causes a release of dopamine in our system. Marketing focuses on the idea of instant gratification because at the heart of it is the impulse to have, change, or purchase something—now. Companies inundate the public with instant messages and communications on our devices, through social media, and on TV, making it easier than ever to purchase new products with a phone or an app. Without delay or even much thought, people have a heightened sense of urgency about products and ideas that are delivered instantaneously.

Neuroeconomics is a relatively new study of the brain's ability to make good decisions that lead you to success. A classic study offered participants $50 now or $100 in a year; those who took the money immediately demonstrated lesser impulse control or greater desire for instant gratification. Recently, this study was redone and recorded in the *Journal of Neuroscience*.[2] In this case the participants had their brains monitored while facing the reward scenarios of $50 now or $100 in a year. What the MRIs demonstrated is that those who took the higher reward considered the question by utilizing the part of the brain that addresses the future (the anterior prefrontal cortex). In an article about the study posted on the *Scientific American* website, entitled "How to Avoid the Temptations of Immediate Gratification," Melanie Bauer notes that this study highlights two areas of "future thought." The first type of future thought is "prospective memory"—this is when you create a memory or reminder regarding future events ("pick up milk on the way home from work")—and the second is "episodic future memory"—this is when you think about and consider future events or actions ("what movie shall I watch tonight?"). But the future is not always entirely clear. Giving more definition to the future thought or idea helps people wait for it, as it engages "episodic future memory" and helps you delay gratification.

By helping your customers better visualize their future experience with you and your company, you may help them delay gratification by helping them think about the future. Thinking about the future utilizes these two areas of future thought, which can help your customers create a goal and memory around the eventual satisfying experience, and in the process they can thwart the impulse of instant gratification. By describing your products and experiences in detail, you may be helping your customers wait to achieve satisfaction. Back to that "medium rare steak." If a server addresses the customer in the moment of complaint and tells him that she will replace the steak, and the steak will be out when it's cooked, you're not doing enough to help the customer feel that satisfaction is assured. However, if the server describes that she will deliver their steak "pink but not too red and fresh off the grill" and then give them a proper time estimate "this should take around 8–10 minutes, let me just confirm with the chef," then she has helped the customer create an expectation of the future experience and establish the idea of future satisfaction in his mind. By creating a "future memory" of satisfaction, you are helping your guests believe in their own eventual satisfaction with our brand and products.

Satisfying Service

The American Customer Satisfaction Index was created in 1994 by researchers at Michigan University and is the only cross-industry measure of customer satisfaction in the United States. The index is based on a number of customer experience benchmarks that include courtesy and helpfulness of staff, website satisfaction, call center satisfaction, ease of understanding information, and ease of making changes as well as more detailed deliverables (e.g., number of ATMs). In various industries the customer rating of call center satisfaction varies. In the category that includes health insurance and banks the call centers were rated at a dismal 68–77 percent. Whereas in the sectors of property and casualty insurance, Internet brokerage, and credit unions, the experience ranged from 82 percent up to 90 percent.

In the most recent index from August 2015 the five top-rated industries on the list are video players and credit unions (86 and 85%) followed by soft drinks, personal care & cleaning products, internet brokerage, internet retail and full service restaurants, all of which ranked at 82 percent. The bottom four industries were Airlines (71%), health insurance (70%), fixed line telephone service (69%) and Public administration/Government (65%) with subscription television service and Internet service providers at the end of the list at a measly score of 63 percent. What this demonstrates is that in no industry sector are businesses able to satisfy their clients 100 percent of the time. How do you deal with all these dissatisfied customers? By understanding that the service you give can make all the difference in the world. It can be the one thing that saves you from your products and your deliverables.

That's right. When things go wrong, service saves the day. Active service makes the biggest impact on customer satisfaction, and there are many things we, as service providers, can do when things go wrong to make things go right. The moment a problem crops up, it presents us with an opportunity to make a quick and memorable solution: immediate attention, a professional approach, and a quick resolution. I always tell my team: "We have so many things to make people happy," and this is the truth. But making people happy requires action, intervention, and communication. These are the "Three Musketeers" of good service.

In the restaurant world it is widely acknowledged that people go out to eat not only to quench hunger and relieve thirst, but first and foremost to feel better. Going out to eat, even at a Subway restaurant, is a treat in customers' minds. As customers, we reward ourselves with many things in a restaurant: delicious food, potent drinks, not having to cook, being served by someone—these all elicit feelings. And feeling *better* is what brings us out every time. What is the emotion when we go get our car serviced? When we go to the dentist? When we go on a website to make a purchase? The emotion is still there and is very much alive and active—even more so when things go wrong.

Throughout my career I have seen time and time again a potential disaster made into a satisfying customer experience. One night, when I was consulting to Le Cirque (a 40-year-old fine dining temple in New York City), there was a couple at a prominent table who was experiencing a break up, a sadly familiar scene. The woman was distraught, the man was stone-faced, and the people seated next to them on both sides were clearly uncomfortable and staring me down with a pleading look that said "*do* something." The initial risk was disturbing the couple in a supremely intimate moment, but the greater risk was the discomfort they were bringing to the three tables that surrounded them. Their collective discomfort was about to turn into a dissatisfying dining experience for everyone involved. I had to come up with a swift and considerate solution.

I approached the distraught woman at the table and softly said "I can see you're upset, I have a nice quiet table in the lounge where you might have more privacy." She accepted the other table and in doing so saved face. The gentleman paid their check and joined his wife, and we sent drinks to the nearby guests. The nearby guests thanked us for offering the suffering couple some relief and privacy and for giving them a much-needed break from the drama—and so did the distraught couple. And by spending some money (sending drinks adds up fast), we replaced the memory of the fighting with one of the resolution. In this scenario everyone left satisfied and with a positive impression of the service received and of Le Cirque.

As a manager, you must act and be creative, but you must also empower your employees to do the same. Conversing with your customer in order to find out what he or she was expecting and what will make this customer feel better is a skill that all companies must develop. When the mistakes are made and dissatisfaction is on the horizon, it is imperative to find out what will lead to the customer's eventual satisfaction. For some people replacement is the key, for some a refund is all it takes. For others, the actions of a caring and competent manager are all it takes to keep the customer happy and satisfied and make the memory of the experience a positive one.

Tips and Takeaways

- **Teach "Happy."** Train your team to give satisfaction to your guests and give team members examples for creating satisfying options for their customers. Making people happy is an art and a skill; it can be learned, and thus it must be taught. Especially if your company is in the business of any sort of "personalized service," you must train your staff on what your expectations of a "happy customer" are and show your employees how to create a personalized experience. Finding out what someone means by "blue" when shopping for paint requires a number of comparisons and examples to derive the blue color the person is seeking. Even creating a financial portfolio is a bespoke service as the financial planner must truly understand his client's appetite for risk and reward. For some "I want to retire well" means having their mortgage paid off and their pension working properly; for others it means ensuring their retirement funds keep them in the lifestyle to which they are accustomed, private jet and all.
- **Find Out For Yourself.** Engage customers to find out what makes them happy and satisfied with your products and services. Elicit feedback in person by asking open questions about your guests' expectations and actual experience. Asking guests to tell you about their experience is made easier when posing open-ended questions, such as "Tell me about your experience at the cashier today" or "Did our service match your expectation, Mrs. Jones?" Truly engaging customers will help you glean insights about the happiness your customers gain from interacting with your business, your products, and your staff.
- **Make Satisfaction Your Mission.** Use the idea of "satisfaction" to inspire your core values and mission. Think about the satisfaction or happiness you want your customers to leave with, and then work backward from there: how can you get to this goal realistically? Posing the question

early in the timeline of building the concept of your business helps you consider the "emotional deliverables" of your business. Satisfaction and happiness are two goals that you must identify and define early on and then provide to every guest you serve.

- **Sharing Pride.** Create a platform for your staff members where they can share customer success stories. It can be in a group chat, a blog, or a notice on an employee bulletin board; it's having a place to crow about your customers' satisfaction. Highlighting customer satisfaction and the part the staff played in it are great ways to live out the goal of the business while also helping your staff members to "walk the walk" of service in your company. Showing pride in delivering a happy experience can help inspire others and creates a lasting story about success in your business: your success is equal to the satisfaction of your customers and staff.

CHAPTER 7

A Little Decency

Obliging and Generous

For a time when I was working at Per Se, I managed the events in the private dining room. Event planners would spend months planning every detail of a high level dinner for their valued guests at this restaurant with three Michelin stars. In turn, my staff and I would spend hours and days preparing for each client; the food, wine, menus, flowers, seating arrangements, and staffing requirements all called for precision and attention to detail to ensure a perfectly executed party.

One event stands out among the hundreds that I oversaw. It was an annual corporate cocktail party with two bars and passed canapés for around 100 people. Guests were greeted with glasses of champagne, and the canapés were miniature versions of some of the famous Thomas Keller dishes. The food at this restaurant was always impeccably served, but on this miniature scale the food looked exquisite. Little jewels served on beautiful, curved forks, lovely little spoons, and in tiny glasses. Gorgeous and incredibly appetizing.

One of the waiters came to me after passing canapés to one guest. The guest shared with him that her jaw was wired shut so she couldn't eat any of the delights being passed around and asked if there was any juice for her to drink. The server got her some juice and after speaking with this guest myself, I discovered that she was desperate to taste the food and would love to try some even if it were pureed. Puréed? We didn't normally purée food in that manner, but I figured I would see what I could work out with the private dining chef.

The chef was excited for a challenge and grabbed the Vitaprep blender. He tossed in a few ingredients, blended them up, and realized the puréed foods tasted pretty good! With some tweaking and ingenuity he sent out a number of small puréed bites for this impaired guest to enjoy. Cold soups, hot soups, and inventive flavor combinations pureed into shakes made this woman's night, and it was so satisfying to observe her getting the chance to experience the flavors that had won the Michelin stars alongside her colleagues. The experience inspired the chef to be innovative and creative and throw caution (purée the food?) to the wind, all for the dining experience of this one-in-a-hundred customer.

The source of everyone's behavior that night was decency. A regular person, enduring an untenable situation, was able to ask for help, and something uncomfortable was turned into an enjoyable experience. She asked us to feed her and rather than saying "We couldn't possible do that, our food is not meant to be consumed that way," we did the decent thing. We were able to have this guest participate in the event rather than look in on it from the outside. And it felt great; we all felt successful and satisfied in doing this simple act.

When I worked at Balthazar, Keith McNally implored us to "just treat people decently," and we tried to show that decency to everyone who came in. So many places strive to be "incredible," "world class," or "amazing," but this is hard to embody and hard to comprehend. These exceptional states are very hard to make actionable. Just what is "incredible" anyway? What I've discovered is that it is hard for your staff to understand how to "be incredible to your guests" all the time, but it is quite easy to show simple human decency toward your guests. In the battle of "incredible" versus "decent," I advocate for the latter every time.

It is important to understand better what true decency is. Recently we have come to equate "decent" with "average," "standard," or "okay," but it actually means much more. As defined by the *New Oxford American Dictionary*, "decent" has a few meanings that are key to the customer service equation:

decent |dēsənt|
adjective

1. conforming with generally accepted standards of respectable or moral behavior: the good name of such a decent and innocent person.
   - appropriate; fitting: they would meet again after a decent interval.
   - not likely to shock or embarrass others: a decent high-necked dress.
2. [attrib.] of an acceptable standard; satisfactory: find me a decent cup of coffee | people need decent homes.
   - good: the deer are small: a 14-inch spread is a pretty decent buck.
   - kind, obliging, or generous: that was pretty awfully decent of him.

To be decent is not about exhibiting average behavior. In fact, the word decent contains the values of being "appropriate," "not likely to embarrass others," "good," and "kind, obliging, or generous." Indeed, these are the hallmarks of amazing service. Examples of amazing service happen all the time: the server running after a customer who has left a credit card behind, a doorman helping a pregnant woman get her shopping bags in her car, airline personnel calling for a wheelchair for an older passenger. All acts of decency that read as "incredible service."

The key to showing decency is that it must be authentic and true to that particular moment. Not every older person requires a wheelchair at the airport and not every pregnant woman is a damsel in distress. In *The Manager's Book of Decencies* Steve Harrison explains how decent behavior can help you build a strong company culture. One of the key aspects of a decent act is that it is unexpected;[1] I believe that the unexpectedness of a decent gesture is what makes it truly incredible. He also says that one of the keys to showing decency in customer service is to remember a small detail about the person you are working with. This is very true; when the person helping you remembers your name, the waiter remembers your drink preference, and the dry cleaner asks after your child's health, you feel good because you have been considered. These little thoughtful gestures add up to customer acknowledgment and go a long way to make the customer service experience a positive one.

No Bartering Allowed

Sophia knows that the small things matter. When calling T-Mobile to upgrade her cell phone to the latest model, she had discovered that her preferred color was out of stock. The associate apologized and said the phone should be back in stock in about a week. A week later Sophia rang back and got the same associate on the line. When Sophia said she was following up to see if a particular phone was in stock, the associate immediately recognized Sophia and said, "You were looking for the gold model, right?" She was and was able to get the model she wanted later that day. Once at the store, Sophia ended up speaking with the manager about how positive her experience with the associate had been. The starting point was the moment of decency: this associate remembered Sophia and in doing so made her feel special and remembered in addition to being satisfied by getting what she wanted: a new phone in the color she preferred. And the associate got acknowledgment from her customer and her manager for a job well done.

What is crucial to being decent, Harrison writes, is that the decent gesture is offered without any expectation of reward. This was true in the above example: the associate didn't expect Sophia to go to her boss to compliment her work but just authentically remembered what her customer wanted. Once a reward is expected, then the gesture becomes a barter transaction—and this is no longer decent but is commerce. When I was a maitre d', people would often thank me for their table when they left the restaurant by offering a handshake and placing a cash tip in my palm at the same time. This was a clear decent gesture that represented "thank you for the table, we enjoyed ourselves," and I appreciated the extra monetary thanks. However, some people would arrive, money in hand, and ask for or flat-out demand, a "nice table when you can" while holding out $20, $30, or even $50. There was no decency in this gesture, it was clearly a barter that represented "I'm paying you for a table, make it nice and snappy." I always handed the money back and said "If you are happy with your experience, you may thank me later." Some people would, some not. But once a reward or a particular outcome is expected, then what made the gesture decent at first has been erased.

The question that you must ask yourself is whether you want your brand and staff to be swayed by monetary incentives. If as maître d' I had a side business of taking tips to give people tables ahead of others, I would have been bartering on my own behalf rather than act on the behalf of the other customers. This makes the salesperson or manager an agent acting on his or her own behalf, not a fair representative of the business. We all know that money talks, but we're talking about decency and service. What is the service experience you want to deliver? When you consider the decent reception of your guests, you will include a lot more people who are there to be engaged by your service rather than trying to strong-arm it.

Aiming Too High

Most managers and owners tell us to strive for excellence, greatness, and incredible results. There is nothing wrong with that, but when people are aiming so high, it is very easy to miss the basics. Small but essentially decent gestures are the ones that speak volumes about your business. For example, looking someone in the eyes, greeting customers by name, showing concern for their distress, and going out of your way to fix their problem are all ways to be decent to strangers, and these gestures all say something about your business in a way no product feature, however incredible, can. By showing decency, you are demonstrating great consideration for your guests, and this is truly incredible.

I am frequently retained to create and develop the mission and core values for my clients' businesses. When I'm in the process of doing so, I create a list of "concepts and words" based on interviews I conduct with the owners and managers. I compile a list of the words I hear people using to describe the business and what it stands for. The most common words people use to describe their business and what it represents are "outstanding," "incredible," "flawless," "amazing." These are all great in theory, but it is impossible to ask someone to "be amazing." There is no textbook example of "amazing" human behavior, and I have found that people don't know what to do when given this directive. I suggest you consider substitute words that are actionable versions of the ones listed above. For example, "outstanding" becomes "special," "amazing" becomes "unexpected," and "incredible" becomes "believable." Then you create the mission and core values using these words and concepts.

For instance, you may speak about creating "unexpected" moments of delight for your customers so that their experience feels amazing. Or you could ask your employees to think about the ways they can tailor their service for that particular client so it can be more "special" and the client perceives it as outstanding. These word choices speak to the actions you can take that will result in a positive feeling that is amazing, outstanding, or incredible. Ultimately, what this process strives to do is to make it easier for the team to embody the mission and core values in their everyday service actions and attitude.

In fact, with the words "special," "unexpected," and "believable," you have the basic definition of decency. And when your mission and core values embody decency, your team will be more able to connect authentically to your customers. In turn, your customers can connect authentically to your brand. I always call the mission of a business "the North Star." A well-crafted mission statement can help you when you make decisions as it keeps you on course by defining what you do every day. The core values of a business are the code staff members use to define their actions as employees. Many times the core values include concepts like "team player," "respect," or "kindness." These are all concepts that your teams can embody and live out in their daily work life.

"Being amazing" does exist. It happens when we see everyday heroes in the news. People who stop what they're doing to help another person, to call 911, to offer assistance, to jump in with action, to offer a shoulder to cry on. These are the actions of regular people we perceive as amazing, incredible, or outstanding. These actions are all offered without thought of reward and are offered naturally and in response to great urgency. In an emergency time is of the essence, but the motivation that leads people to do great things is the same: empathy for the other person, consideration for the person in front of you, commiseration with a fellow human being. And this leads to acts of decency that offer so much.

Decency is what people want after all and not only when they are in a tough situation. Decency is what people talk about when talking about the best service they have received. When people comment on their positive service experiences, they offer similar responses, for example:

"I felt so comfortable."
"They understood my needs."

"I felt heard."

"They offered a swift solution."

"They were thoughtful of my time."

These good feelings were generated because of what a salesperson did. What he or she did was follow through, listen, respond on time, be friendly, and offer help.

Unfortunately, the opposite often happens, and judgment is just what some customers have come to expect. Many businesses strive to be non-judgmental, but there are common situations that lead many staff members to judge the people in front of them based, for example, on the way these people dress, the way they wear their hair, their body language, and the culture or knowledge they express. Very often employees are quick to sum up strangers and make decisions about them as potential customers based on only superficial clues. Some of the most highly regarded people in our society don't always demonstrate their status through their clothing or appearance. Oprah was famously denied entrance to a shop in Paris ostensibly because no one recognized her as being Oprah or a person who might shop in the store. Imagine if you are not Oprah and want to go shopping in a high-end shop, you may feel insecure about being taken seriously and treated as a legitimate customer.

I regularly hear stories of people who feel insecure about shopping at certain stores, eating at certain restaurants, and going to certain gyms. They are insecure about fitting in or being treated with respect because they look or appear different. This is where decency is lacking. Think about your business. Does it feel exclusive? Is your staff trained to approach certain types of customers based on their appearance, clothing, or language? If your team members are tuned in to one way of discovering a customer, then you must open their minds to the most decent way of discovering customers: by being open to everyone who comes in. This way you will avoid the pitfalls of judgment and just may invite a person who didn't consider herself a customer at first into becoming a valued and loyal guest.

Comfort is a physical feature that is manifested in the environment of the business. A business makes guests comfortable and puts them "at ease" by being communicative, helpful, timely, friendly, and nonjudgmental. "At ease" is defined as being "free from worry, awkwardness, or problems" in the *New Oxford American Dictionary*. This is what you want all of your guests to feel in your business; a worried guest who is expecting an awkward or problematic experience will be harder to woo. However, many guests arrive at doorstep of a business worried and stressed.

My second-most memorable guest at Per Se was the classical cellist Yo Yo Ma. He and his wife were warm, gracious, outgoing and humble and presented themselves immaculately. They fit the picture of a guest of this restaurant: internationally poised, comfortable in the luxury environment, and finely attired. My *most* memorable guests, however, did not fit the usual mold. It was a couple from Pennsylvania, dressed modestly and clearly nervous and out of place in the dining room. I sensed their unease and went to greet them; I introduced myself and asked if they had any questions about the menu. Once I engaged them, they told me a touching story. The couple loved food and cooking, and it was their life's dream to eat at a Thomas Keller restaurant. They had read about the French Laundry and had seen the cookbooks in bookstores and literally saved their pennies to afford the meal they were about to enjoy. They had saved enough to pay for two prix-fixe menus, no additions and no beverages. They could only afford to drink iced water. Their extra money was for gas and parking, and they couldn't believe they were actually sitting in this storied dining room.

Their story and palpable delight at achieving their dream touched me, and I asked the chef if we could send them some extra courses and basically give them the VIP treatment. Once the courses started coming to the table, the couple was astonished and delighted at the food they were eating and the experience they were sharing. I told them that we wanted them to have a memorable experience and this evidently touched them as well. They looked at one another, and with tears in their eyes told me that the husband was ill and this might be the last time they would be able to have this experience, as his recovery would be intense and lengthy. At this point, tears came to my eyes as well. By sharing their dream with me and the staff helping to make it come true, we were all part of a significant moment in their lives. This was not just dinner, this was a lifelong dream achieved.

Before they left, I took them on a tour of the kitchen and had a bag of chocolates waiting for them at the door. They took time to shake the cook's hands, give thanks to the team, and left me with a heartfelt hug. They stayed in my memory for a very long time: they were the most humble and deserving guests I have ever encountered, and it was truly a pleasure to serve them. By treating them like one of our most valued guests and offering them our expanded service, we made an impact on two strangers who have remained in my memory and heart for many years. Decency was the hero, and a dream dinner was the reward.

I Hear You

I have established that "service is a conversation" and that a conversation is the way to understand your guests and begin to build trust with them. First by engaging them, then listening, then suggesting, then selling. The sale will be made in a way that feels like consideration rather than like a hard-core sale and in the end this is what all businesses should strive for: to give guests what they want. That is, selling must be done with a light touch, and this is an aspect of selling that you must address in staff training. There must be give and take, and good service is all about communication: listening, asking questions, and then offering advice, information, or answers based on what you hear.

Executive coaches often utilize open-ended questions to help a client identify what is at the root of their issue. Open-ended questions often start with "what," "when," "who," "where," or "how" to evoke a thoughtful response. "What are you looking for today?" is a great open-ended question to start a service conversation. "How may I help you?" is a typical opening line in many service scripts because it is open and invites the other person into a conversation. One questioning word that might get a different response is "why." "Why" puts people on the defensive and shines a light on them by asking them to provide an excuse or an explanation. "Why" is probing and can appear too personal. Therefore, in place of "why did you do that?" you might use "how did you come to that decision?" or "what influenced your decision?" "Why" puts the focus on the person whereas "how" or "what" put the focus on the decision or thought, thus taking the sting out of a direct "why."

Active listening is a technique in which the listener gives feedback to the speaker by repeating back what the speaker originally said. With this technique the listener utilizes questions to indicate that they are hearing what the speaker is saying to them. Questions allow the listener to narrow down the request or the complaint and then lets the speaker feel heard and understood. This is especially helpful when a customer is distraught, confused, or upset. For instance, active listening would go something like this:

Customer: I don't like the snowblower I just bought. I want to return it.

Salesperson: Oh no, I'm sorry to hear that. What happened?

Customer: I got it home, filled it with gas, and it wouldn't start. And now my driveway is a mess! I'm really annoyed.

Salesperson: That sounds really annoying; it is a nasty day. I'm really sorry to hear it. So you set it up and filled it with gas, and then it didn't turn over, right?

Customer: Yeah, I just filled it up with gas. But it did turn over. It just didn't start.

Salesperson: So it wasn't completely dead, correct?

Customer: Right.

Salesperson: Maybe the engine was flooded. Would you be open to having one of our repairmen look at it? If you have a moment, I'll see if I can get someone to look at it now? This might be a quick fix, and then you can clear your driveway today. Otherwise I can do a return. Did you bring your receipt?

Customer: I have my receipt. I just want this one to work, can you get someone to look at it? That would be great, it's in the back of my truck.

In this example the listener was able to get more information from the customer and offer a quick fix that really gives the customer what he or she wants: a working snowblower. Active listening, asking open questions, and then narrowing down the problem led the listener to a great solution. Too often customers experience listening that is not active and does not repeat the information received; this kind of listening doesn't get to the root of the problem.

When you listen actively and attentively, you are exhibiting decency. When you employ active listening techniques, you can offer a solution your customer can be happy with. Active listening is also important when making a sale; with more information, the salesperson can better serve his customer's need. But often salespeople veer away from listening in order to sell by way of lecturing. When you are lecturing, you are no longer having a conversation; listening has stopped, and decency has just left the building. Pay attention to those staff members who give soliloquies or long-winded lectures on the advantages of one product over another. This is not a conversation, and the feeling lecturing elicits is that "they don't care about me, they just want to talk." Never underestimate the power of listening; it can transform your business.

Extending decency to your customers is actually pretty easy. Listening, following up, and being on time are all behaviors that can be learned or taught and are completely free of charge. And these are the little things that push businesses to the top of the Yelp leaderboard and generate reviews with the highest ratings. But not every situation is a success. How do your employees show decency when there is a two-hour wait, when a reservation is lost, and the birthday is overlooked? By being thoughtful, actively listening and treating your customers with concern and with empathy. These decent actions will resonate in the mind of your guest and help them feel better about their experience. It is truly amazing what you can accomplish with honesty, genuine kindness, a smile, optimism, and action.

Tips and Takeaways

- **Consistency Counts**. You must always demonstrate decency with all of your guests. Even if someone appears "unusual," you must keep your poise and treat that person the same respect as any other customer. Caution your team against making comments or making fun of someone who is different or unconventional. Your lead will show the way, and your ability to offer decency to someone unique will get the attention of your staff members and help them stay the course of kindness.

- **Start with Your Staff.** Utilize active listening and employ open-ended questions in staff interactions in order to understand your employees' experience a bit better. Encourage active listening with your management team and take time to listen in to manager/staff interactions to ensure people are utilizing this method. And as always, remind yourself to be open and refrain from pigeonholing others when speaking with them. Your team can tell you a lot about your business if you listen and engage with team members on a regular basis; good listening will expand these moments nicely.

- **Celebrate Decency.** Create a decency touchpoint for company newsletters, meetings, and communication. Ask your team members to consider how they can impact guests' experience by being "kind, obliging, or generous." Acknowledge the team that celebrates the little decencies: for example, helping people with their bags, offering additional information, assisting with a quandary outside your business (when someone's car has been towed, for example). Each of these examples offers a way to impact a guest's experience that will be memorable and incredible when offered freely and with genuine humanity.

- **Find the Balance.** Use your guest surveys to ask about areas of "decency" that could be improved. Are the cashiers so efficient that your guests feel rushed out the door? Try and find a balance between throughput (moving people through the process) and a more considerate approach. Ask your cashiers to consider the customer in front of them, the person's needs and situation. In short, ask them to demonstrate decency and see whether your customers' comments about your business become more favorable.

CHAPTER 8

From Dust to Mistrust

The Wrong Kind of Memory

Staying at a five-star hotel is an amazing experience. The way the entrance curves gently toward the front door and the valets bounce up to your car with grace and a smile makes you feel like royalty. Marble passageways, double height ceilings, and the gracious and grand scale of the place all elicit feelings of awe, inspiration, and marvel. The attention that is put into every little detail is apparent; the lobby seating is arranged just so with the pillows all perfectly plump, and the place smells heavenly. The floral displays, lush and exotic, help guests transcend their ordinary day and feel transported to another, gorgeous world. The staff members, in their impeccable uniforms, greet you by name, help you with your things, and put you at ease; they are neither too obtrusive nor too reserved. But the main event is your room.

The front desk clerk gives you your key with a smile and instructs the bellman to escort you upstairs. He makes small talk and makes you feel welcome in your destination. You arrive at the room, and he opens the door and invites you to enter. The lighting is subtle, the air is cool, and the linens are spotless. The bellman puts your luggage on a stand and shows you the TV remote and how to use the automatic window shades, and before departing he offers to get you anything else, but what else do you need? You're in the lap of luxury.

Until you discover a hair in the bathroom sink. One simple hair, ordinary in itself, is enough for the entire experience to come to a crashing halt.

In this luxurious and detailed world, in your safe and beautiful room, you now feel...unsure. Is there anything else to discover? And now, rather than relaxing, you examine the glasses for cleanliness, the mirror for fingerprints, and the duvet for imperfections. You have begun to doubt your experience because of an errant hair. This little tiny visual message is all you need to tell you that no matter how impressive this place may be, your expectations for luxury and cleanliness have just been permanently lowered.

Cleanliness is a one of the harbingers of service. When a business is clean, well maintained, and tidy, customers feel at ease in the space and are more willing to trust that the experience will be good. Untidy, disorganized, and dirty businesses give us a heads-up that things might not be right; anything that is out of place can preclude any other positive impressions being made. Cleanliness is also a part of making memories as it is elemental and obvious; lack of it can distract customers from an otherwise pleasant experience. A dirty or smelly background affects your guests' memory of the service they will experience.

There are many obvious things in a business that can impact the guest experience, but some are quite subtle. Cleanliness and maintenance offer important cues to your guests and will invite them to believe in your business or beg them to mistrust it. In restaurants and on cruise ships one of the big aspects of customer confidence is cleanliness; in fact, anything less than absolutely sanitary can get you closed down. But cleanliness impacts other businesses more than most people would imagine and will certainly alter guests' decision to return or to spend money again. Cleanliness is one of the important details of service, and your ability to uphold cleanliness is essential to ensuring customers' confidence in your brand.

There are many businesses that are judged harshly for cleanliness; restaurants, hospitals, and cruise ships among them. In these businesses the word itself is replaced by stricter and more industrial terms such as "sanitary," "hygienic," "healthful," and "antiseptic." Cleanliness has an incredible impact on the customer experience, and in 2011, Cintas, a corporate uniform company, went out to prove it. A study conducted on behalf of the company by Harris Interactive revealed that cleanliness was one of the biggest factors in influencing a customer to return to a retail operation. As many as

99 percent of adults surveyed said that cleanliness would affect their perception of the brand they were buying, and it would affect their interest in returning. The top issues affecting customers were:

Unclean restrooms	95 percent
Unpleasant odor	92 percent
Poor customer service	90 percent
Dirty floors	86 percent
Dirty shopping carts	84 percent
Poor staff appearance	83 percent
Spills or stains	81 percent
Wet floors with no signage	76 percent
Dusty surfaces	74 percent
Dirty glasses and windows	68 percent

With poor customer service coming in at a relatively tame 90 percent, what most impacts the customer experience is cleanliness. Customers notice and value a clean business from the floor to the windows to the restrooms. But it is important to note that the appearance of the staff makes an impact as well. Your employees represent your brand, and how they dress, maintain their uniform, and attend to personal grooming is essential to your success. And to the impression of service as a whole.

Your guests will never actually know how clean and sanitized your place is; they will not check for bacterial levels or wipe a shelf with a white glove. But they will use all of their senses in order to determine whether a place is clean or dirty. The visuals of cleanliness are incredibly important. In restaurants at the beginning of dinner service the staff members are regularly tasked with "detailing their sections," which means to buff the glassware and polish the silverware on the set tables in preparation for service. This is a ritual that tells a story of cleanliness: the restaurant is getting ready for its guests by cleaning for them. This is a powerful visual and sends an important message by demonstrating the cleaning process.

Some cleaning should be behind closed doors; removing bags of trash is an act that no one wants to observe. But there are some cleaning moments that tell a story to your clients that can be very positive. Harmony Trujillo, the co-owner of York Building Services, a commercial cleaning company, says that when doing some cleaning for her condo clients, some things are best to do during the hours when people will observe the work being done. "If there is a stain on the carpet," she says, "I like to have my team clean this during the morning hours between 8 and 10 a.m. so that the residents can see the effort that is going into the maintenance of their building. If they don't see the work being done, it is left to their imaginations...and people have all sorts of subjective ideas about cleaning."

Cleaning and the level of cleanliness in your building or business are completely subjective to the person experiencing it. Nothing tells the truth like the action of cleaning a stain on a carpet. It is a nice example of the principle of "I notice = I care"; it tells a story about how the cleaning is performed and serves to fill in the blanks, leaving nothing to the imagination. Some folks will imagine that the cleaning is limited to a quick dusting and the occasional vacuuming. So when people observe the practice of cleaning—washing windows, polishing brass, and cleaning chandeliers—the message of cleanliness is clear: clean, fresh, and sparkling.

Quality Control

In 2001 Gallup conducted a patient survey in order to determine what "quality" meant to patients in a hospital. It turned out that cleanliness was one of the top metrics of quality in a hospital, where "satisfaction with cleanliness" often superseded the patients' overall level of satisfaction with their experience. In an article entitled "Do Patients Equate Cleanliness with Quality?"[1] posted on the Gallup website, Dr. Rick Blizzard addressed these findings by noting that in hospitals the perception of cleanliness is more important than the actual level of cleanliness. Blizzard, a hospital consultant, offers three ways to stay on top of cleanliness that are universally insightful. He insists that cleanliness is assured when you hire and reward talent rather than making "housekeeping" an entry-level position. He also reminds readers that "cleanliness is a perception" and that disorganization in a hallway or marks on a wall will give the perception that things are unclean when in fact they may be completely sanitized. His third tip is to look at things from the "patient's perspective." He says that often in a hospital the employees walk around looking at the floor; however, the patients lying in a bed or on a gurney are not looking at the floor but at the ceiling. It is essential to look at cleanliness from your customers' perspective.

Blizzard calls cleanliness a "dissatisfier: an attribute that can negatively affect perceptions of an otherwise satisfying experience." The term "dissatisfier" is a great buzzword as it highlights how cleanliness can affect customers' otherwise positive impression. Satisfaction is our daily goal, so we must watch out for anything that "dissatisfies" a customer in any way. I maintain that cleanliness is a key element of service as it echoes any good or bad feelings about the service experience and becomes a "halo" of perception. Cleanliness either corroborates the customer's feelings or acts as a warning: the clean bathroom substantiates customers' trust in the business whereas the dirty bathroom adds a question mark where there once was assurance; this keeps the door open for more bad feelings and experiences to come in.

In 2010 an infestation problem of epic proportions hit dozens of offices and stores in every major city in the United States. Bedbugs were appearing everywhere from popular apparel stores to movie theaters to trendy hotels. But they were also discovered in law offices, insurance companies, banks, and accounting firms, much to their clients' horror. Nothing says "dirty" like a bug or rodent infestation and bedbugs are at the top of the list of the most loathed and reviled bugs as they permeate furniture, bite skin, and are hard to eradicate. The MetLife Building on Park Avenue was plagued with the bugs that showed up in various businesses on every floor of this posh address. Bedbugs are even more ominous as they travel from location to location by attaching themselves to clothing, handbags, and suitcases, and they can set up a home in pretty much any type of furniture where there are warm bodies nearby. A bed is great, but a sofa, chair, or carpet is all it takes to make a bedbug feel at home.

While bedbugs are thought to be creepy little insects, the bigger threat is the perception of uncleanliness that they impart. While your business might be clean and sanitized, any kind of bug sighting will send the message of "unclean" to your customers. Ants, spiders, and even mosquitoes can send a message to your customers about cleanliness, sanitation, and maintenance. When I consulted for a resort in the Caribbean, every public bathroom was stocked with Off bug spray due to the overwhelming number of mosquitoes on the property. The housekeeping team did a great job of keeping the mosquitoes at bay in the public areas and limited them to being a nuisance rather than an infestation. In a beachfront resort mosquitoes are pretty much expected, but how you handle them says a lot about how you maintain your property. Cobwebs, dead bugs on the ground, and any sort of insect feces left behind are all indications that the business is losing the war against the pests. The danger of bedbugs or spiders or mosquitoes is that they have nothing to do with cleanliness at all. But what they inspire is a queasy, uneasy feeling that is hard for people to overcome.

Cleanliness is a pipeline of trust. When the operation is sparkling, fresh smelling, and well maintained, your customers will have an easier time trusting your business. When there is dust on the plants, fingerprints on the glass door, and a musty odor filling the air, trust has been compromised. Cleaning is restorative to a business, and it is a necessary daily task.

Germs are among the most feared organisms in the world. Humans fear germs like nothing else, and our culture has adopted antibacterial wipes, hand sanitizers, and disinfectant soaps as the saviors of our species. Hand sanitizers are offered in most offices, many hotels, all hospitals, airports, and schools. Grocery stores now feature sanitizing stations equipped with disinfectant wipes for cleaning grocery carts before and after shopping. Health Clubs and gyms offer sanitizing sprays and wipes for cleaning the equipment before and after members work out. Purell has become the standard offering in so many places because it acts as a calmative for our worst fears: picking up some random germ and getting sick. The obsession with hand sanitizers is a trend that is interesting to observe. Harmony Truillo of York Building Services says that more than ever her office and school clients want Purell dispensers installed in their workplaces. This is both for their own comfort and for the comfort of their staff. But it also offers peace of mind for their customers—office workers, teachers, parents, and students.

Trujillo knows only too well that her clients' workplaces are clean as she oversees the work herself. Her team members do their research to combat the season's biggest threats in order to properly disinfect surfaces to protect against various viruses. "The bathrooms are always the most clean place in any workplace as they get cleaned regularly," Trujillo shared. "We focus on the areas that don't get as much attention but are the places where germs lurk: doorknobs, light switches, the front edges of desks and tables and on computer keyboards." Still, she notes that nothing says "clean" like the Purell dispenser at the front desk, as it also offers the customers control over their own perceived cleanliness. They may not see the effort and cleansing agents used in overnight cleaning, so being offered Purell sanitizer gives customers and clients a feeling of well-being and control over their health and wellness. And the feeling of well-being is what we want our customers to feel when they are doing business with us.

How Sweet It Is

Just look at any poor reviews on Yelp or Trip Advisor, and commonly these reviewers are highlighting businesses that are dirty, dusty, and smelly. With "bad odors" affecting 91 percent of customers in the Cintas study, and reviews that include words like "musty", "stale", "smelly" or "nasty" used to describe businesses as varied as car rental companies, offices of notaries public, health clubs, and even top-name retail stores, it's clear that this is a widespread issue. Other colorful descriptors of poorly rated businesses include "disorganized and dirty," "moldy," "not well maintained," and, memorably, "the ladies' room is gross, it is in need of a good scrubbing." The frustrating challenge with complaints about cleanliness is that it is largely correctable. Washing, cleaning, and sanitizing are universally known to be hard work but work that produces visible results.

One industry that has been increasing in profitability over the years is the cleaning industry. Industrial cleaning companies, corporate cleaners, and even residential cleaning companies have grown steadily due to the increasing demand for their services. In addition, this is a task that fewer businesses want to oversee. In outsourcing the work to a company that focuses solely on cleaning, businesses are assured of receiving a better result for the money spent on cleaning. These crews often work at night so that the business is clean and ready for the staff and customers when it opens the next day. This is another way to improve employee retention and satisfaction and thus improve the bottom line of your business.

While being green is a trend that has become a way of life for many people and businesses, there is a downside. The fresh chemical fragrances usually added to cleaning agents are often removed from green cleaners in order to make the product less harmful for the environment. This makes sense and is a healthful choice. Trujillo's private school clients all insist on using green products in order to make the schools a more habitable environment for the many children with respiratory disorders. However, the teachers frequently complain that the classrooms and bathroom do not smell fresh and clean. They smell neutral, neither bad nor especially clean. The teachers' perception is that the school has not been effectively cleaned, and they often complain that things are not clean when in fact they are. This is a challenge for Trujillo as she strives to deliver a safe and hygienic environment for the children and also wants to assure the teachers that their workplace is clean. She has learned to spray a natural citrus air freshener in the spaces the teachers use in order to send the message of "clean" via their sense of smell.

Our sense of smell is especially important when it comes to creating memories. "Olfactory memory" refers to the way we remember things based on the odors we inhaled and associating them with our experience at the time. Much like the shower curtain smell I mentioned in chapter 2, any smell can make our memories all the more vivid and rich. The olfactory nerve is located very close to the hippocampus, which is the part of our brain that creates memory. It has been shown that when trying to remember or memorize something one should also have a distinctive scent in the room because we then associate the topic learned with the scent we inhale.

If scents make memories all the more intense, then businesses must be more diligent than ever to create fresh smelling environments for their customers and clients. A classic method in restaurants to get people in the mood to eat is to fry some garlic at the beginning of service to fill the restaurant with a good food fragrance. Or to freshen up a dining room brew a big pot of fresh mint in boiling water in order to fill the room with smells associated with food, herbs, and nature. This is a conscious way to influence positive memories in your guests.

Just as delicious odors can influence spending, inappropriate odors can do the opposite. While the teachers at the private school wanted to smell something fresh and clean, certain clean odors don't belong in certain environments. In a restaurant the smell of bleach is not the scent you want your customers to smell although in a hospital it is a reassuring smell that imparts a feeling of cleanliness. Clean scents can be lemon or lavender, but you must make sure that the one you use is in alignment with your brand and service experience. In some instances the scent of lavender can smell fresh and elegant, like a garden in Provence, while in others it can smell too floral and grandmotherly. Similarly, citrus can smell clean and fresh like sunshine while in other environments it can smell sweet and sickly.

Years ago I went to a dingy "down home" restaurant in Manhattan called Princess Pamela's Southern Touch; a restaurant known for its eccentric owner who was the cook (and a cookbook author) and house chanteuse. It was a truly unique night with great music and tasty food; however, the place did not smell fresh. I walked out of there with my clothes permeated with such a strong smell of grease that my clothes needed to be washed twice to remove the rancid smell. This stayed in my memory and prevented me from going back because the place smelled filthy, and I left *feeling* filthy. The restaurant created a big memory of rancid odors but no memory of a desirable service experience. Cleanliness or the lack of it will make a lasting impression on your guests.

Next to Godliness

Because cleanliness can have a huge impact on your business, it is important that you proactively address how clean your business is. One way to do this is to follow Dr. Blizzard's three considerations (value and reward your cleaning team, understand that cleanliness is a perception, and look at things from your customers' perspective) and another way is to use the "5 S" technique. The 5 S technique is a workplace organization method originally developed in Japan as a thoughtful and easy method for keeping a workplace in top shape.

The first S is "sort" and it sets the stage for organization as it forces you to get rid of outdated or unneeded things and focus on those items that are most important. The second S, "set in order," refers to having a place for everything and everything in its place. A sense of order or organization adds to the perception that things are clean; your customers' ability to find what they need is essential to selling products

"Shine," the third S, is the hallmark of cleanliness as it asks your team to evaluate the cleanliness of everything under your roof, address it by cleaning or maintaining it, and ensure there are products in place for keeping up with this daily task. The fourth S is "standardize," which inspires you to develop systems and standards for addressing cleanliness and methods for making it easy for your team to achieve and maintain those standards. The last S is "sustain," and this is the key to the equation as cleanliness is something that must be accomplished daily, weekly, and monthly and with each client. In a hair salon or a doctor's office cleaning happens multiple times a day and there must be a good system in place for cleaning the chair or room after each client has finished and before a new client arrives.

The physical upkeep of the facility can enhance or detract from the trust customers put in your business. Trust is the unspoken but obvious currency in any business transaction. If everything seems in order, is clean and smells good then it will be easier for your customers to trust your business. But when they have poor impressions of your business based on a facility that is unclean, unsanitary or disorganized, your customer can't help but distrust the entire enterprise.

Tips and Takeaways

- **Cleanliness Starts Outside the Business**. Ensure that the entrance, windows, awning, and approach to the business are all attended to regularly and are spiffy and clean. The wrong impression can be all too easily made by a lawn that is unkempt, the overflowing ashtray, the bird droppings on the awning, or the trash in the gutter in front of your place. All tell a story about noticing, and as always, you must notice first.

- **Look Around**. As a client once said to me "If you start stepping over the cigarette butt, that tells me you're slipping." In short, if you start ignoring the mess, your team will as well. Conduct regular uniform checks, ensuring that everyone looks and dresses the part and looks impeccable. The manager's attention to his or her own appearance tells a story about your business; they are closely linked. And make sure that no one is wearing too much cologne; your guests' senses should not be distracted by overpowering perfume fragrance from noticing the fresh, clean, and appropriate odors of your business.

- **Keep a Record**. Keep a deep cleaning log for tracking professional cleaning projects that need attention from time to time. Deep cleaning the carpets, power washing the fences, cleaning out the drain pipes are all regular cleaning duties that you want people to notice and register. More eyes, in this case, make light work.

- **Take a Peek**. There are some customer areas that you must keep track of regularly. If there are customer bathrooms and employee bathrooms, make sure that someone from your management team regularly checks the guest bathrooms to ensure the area is clean and well stocked. Ensure that customer changing rooms are regularly swept or swiffed to keep the floors clean and that merchandise is returned to the sales floor. Guest transportation matters too; the elevators, vehicles, or stairwells that are for "guests only" must be checked regularly for cleanliness and order.

CHAPTER 9

What Brings Regulars Back

Creatures of Habit

When I worked at Balthazar we had hundreds of regulars. Those who came daily for breakfast or lunch, those who came weekly the same night every week, those who came monthly, and those who showed up with varying frequency at breakfast, lunch, or dinner. We had regulars at the bar, regulars in the bakery, and regulars who would order a cup of coffee in the morning and stay for hours. I remember during my waitressing years I had a regular who was in real estate. He and his girlfriend would come once or twice a week, sit at the same table, and without fail, he would order the same thing. To this day I can remember his order:

- Stoli Ohranj, on the rocks
- 12 kumamoto oysters
- Chicken Riesling (when this was off the menu—it was a seasonal item and served only in the winter—it would spark a conversation about his dismay and horror that it was off the menu. Every year. Like clockwork.)
- Red wine, usually a Rhone red. This was the one thing that changed.
- Otherwise it was more Stoli Ohranj

He was completely reliable as a guest because he always ordered the same thing. I'm quite certain he would be shocked to hear that I remember his order after all these years, but more than that I imagine he would be shocked to hear that he was so consistent. Literally, he was a creature of habit.

Every customer at Balthazar wanted to call himself or herself a "regular" of the restaurant mainly because the restaurant projected that kind of atmosphere. On any night we would have guests who had dined with us 50–150 times—that is, they were truly regulars—and then we had guests who had joined us a mere 3 times over the same seven-year period. What I always found interesting is that people who came in once a year for a birthday or some special occasion made a big deal of "being a regular" at the restaurant. Of course, they were hardly "regular" compared to the weekly guests. But having a place to go, even once a year, had meaning to them; they would call the restaurant "their place," with words like "favorite" or "the best" peppering their descriptions to their guests. It seems that being a regular is something that people seek out and take pride in whether it is on a small or large scale.

Being a regular is about being consistent. Going any place with regularity, whether it is a coffee shop, car wash, or summer vacation spot is something people like to do. There is a rhythm to having a regular place to visit, and having a go-to spot generally makes life easier. Jeremy Miller of Sticky Marketing writes on his blog that consistency is a habit that makes things easier. When things in our lives are consistent, then we have to think less, and this is a good thing.

He illuminates his daily drive to work: it is so consistent he barely remembers making the trip at all because the route, the speed, and the time of day are the same. And this lack of effort is a positive because it is one less thing to think about. We all love the comfort of these daily habits, and the consistency of them makes them all the more pleasing. He says that McDonald's has designed its stores with consistency in mind, with each store offering the same colors, lighting, menu, queues, and timing. It is a way to inspire comfort in the store because you don't have to make any new decisions about your meal, and the habit you formed in one location can be applied to this new one. The habit and the reliable nature of that habit, is so comforting that people will go out of their way to seek it out.

This explains the once-a-year regulars. They have built a habit that once a year, on their special day, they can go to this restaurant and have a great time. They know they will feel good about it because they are comfortable; the habit has been built, and there are no new decisions to make. And at Balthazar we delivered the same experience again and again.

On the flip side, Miller makes the point that inconsistency "creates dissonance," and this leads to dissatisfaction with the brand. Think about this scenario: a salesperson has made a great pitch, sold the product well, and made the sale; the customer wants to check something out about his new purchase and goes to the product website, and the website is outdated and hard to navigate. A dissonance has occurred, and the trust this customer had in the company has been put in doubt. The salesperson's positive pitch has now been tainted by the inconsistency of the brand representation online. When there are inconsistencies, your client's brain has to work harder and make decisions about your business. "Can I trust this company? Should I continue this relationship? Is this website reliable?" You don't want your customers to doubt you, you want to make them happy and feel good about doing business with your company.

You must work to develop your regulars and give them reasons to return. Loyalty programs are designed to do just that with the best programs offering free products, discounts, and trial sizes designed to lure guests back and reward them for their patronage. Some of the best loyalty programs also consider what makes the process of returning to the store or the site that much easier. For example, Starbucks has created a payment app that makes it easy for customers to pay for their purchases by using their smartphone. The app also tracks spending and automatically notes that when the tenth beverage is ordered it is free. Starbucks knows that by making it easy for customers to pay the company is making it easier for them to return, helping to build the habit of patronizing Starbucks. This is the regular guest you want: the guest who has built a habit around our business.

Superloyal Guests

In the mid 1890s just outside Lausanne, Switzerland, a man was in his garden, counting his peas. The gentleman, Vilfredo Pareto—an economist, engineer, sociologist, and philosopher—observed that 80 percent of his peas came from

20 percent of his peapods. This got him thinking. In his studies he noticed that it was not just peas that followed this pattern, but many natural phenomena did so as well. As his hypothesis developed, he also found that his theory applied to land ownership and the wealth of citizens throughout Italy. Pareto discovered that 80 percent of the land in Italy was owned by 20 percent of the people, and in 1896 he published a paper that detailed this theory. The theory is now referred to as the Pareto principle; essentially, the theory says that 80 percent of results come from 20 percent of effort. Applied to business, this means that 80 percent of your sales are generated by 20 percent of your clients. This is very valuable information.

You want to cultivate regulars. You want to capture those first-timers and make them come back. If 20 percent of your guests can generate so much revenue for your business, then you must consider what makes a regular a regular. Your regulars are having an impact on your bottom line and on your business as a whole; they talk up your business and take pride in it. And what turns a regular customer into a regular is something you can impact.

Thanx is a loyalty program provider that works for both the customer and the merchant. Thanx has developed an app that is connected to customers' credit cards and tracks their spending (aka loyalty) through their payments to various companies that are subscribers to the Thanx merchant program. This becomes an easy way to track and acknowledge customers' loyalty to various merchants and allows merchants to do away with loyalty cards altogether. Thanx has become very insightful in its analytics, and in 2014 the company published a study of anonymous data from 54 of their merchants that included data from 10.3 million customers and 18.3 million transactions over a six-month period. The findings shared in the study entitled "6 Critical Stats for Customer Loyalty," are very insightful.[1]

Thanx was essentially able to prove the 80/20 rule and make it more concrete through the lens of real sales. The company's findings showed that 64 percent of revenue is generated by 25 percent of customers overall. But there is a split: among restaurant clients the revenue generated by the top 25 percent of customers was 59 percent, and in retail businesses the number went up to 72 percent. This makes the top 25 percent of retail customers all the more important because they generate almost ¾ of stores' total sales.

Thanx advises businesses to discover and track top spenders and identify VIPs to ensure they are always given a reason to return to the business. Thanx also found that only 3 percent of loyal customers are "superloyal," which means they shop monthly, compared to 70 percent of customers who are considered at risk, which means they were loyal once but haven't returned in the last four months. It is critical that you continue to inspire your customers, coaxing them from an infrequent guest into a loyalty star.

Another insight Thanx offers is that spending occurs with different frequency on different days of the week, and 49 percent of repeat shoppers spend money on the weekends while 12 percent spend on Monday through Friday. This presents the opportunity to try and lure these regular guests back more often on the weekdays by offering incentives and deals. Another consideration is to try and lure your loyal guests from one location to visit your other locations. As the above-mentioned showed, 77 percent of customers frequent one location whereas 23 percent frequent multiple locations. And if you can inspire your loyal guests to check out a new location, you have discovered that they are truly loyal and are perhaps your superloyal clients to cultivate and keep.

What People Want

What you want are regular, loyal, consistent customers; customers who have already decided they love your business and who have built a habit with your company. What your customers want is to patronize a consistent business; one that doesn't make them think too much so that they can build a habit with that company. Your customers want the same thing from you that you want from them: consistency.

With *Influence: The Power of Persuasion* Robert B. Cialdini has created a masterpiece of a marketing book. Written in 1984, the book is highly regarded not only for its marketing insights but also it highlights the intricacies of the human psyche. In the book Cialdini highlights the various ways people can influence others, and his thoughts on consistency are revealing. He explains that inconsistency is not a valued personality trait but can be construed as "indecisive, confused, two-faced, or even mentally ill."[2] But consistency is just the opposite and is associated with "personal and intellectual strength [and] is at the heart of logic, rationality, stability, and honesty."[3] With all these positive associations it is no wonder that people strive to be consistent and demonstrate consistency through their actions.

In his book Cialdini highlights a study conducted at a racetrack where people who placed bets were more confident in their choice after putting down money on a certain horse than before they made the bet. This was due to consistency. Turns out people have a deep-seated need to demonstrate consistency to others, and once people place money on a horse based on a mere feeling, they will do what they can to uphold their hunch and demonstrate that it has real meaning. If they were to put $20 on a racehorse without this confidence, then they might appear inconsistent. And people do not want to appear inconsistent because of all its troublesome associations. "Once we have made a choice or taken a stand, we will encounter personal and interpersonal pressures to behave consistently with that commitment. Those pressures will cause us to respond in ways that justify our earlier decision."[4] This explains why people stay on a diet that doesn't work or stay with a boyfriend or girlfriend who isn't particularly nice to them. It is important for us to justify and stand up for our choices in order to be considered and feel consistent.

The key to consistent behavior is commitment. Commitment is widely studied by social psychologists because it is the reason we have such long-standing dedication to a brand or idea. When we make a commitment of any kind, we find even bigger commitments easier, and as we make those, so we have become consistent in our actions. This is seen as a positive trait. Salespeople know this is true, and some sales pitches are designed to get consumers to purchase, even the smallest purchase possible, because it is an entry-level commitment to the brand or business. Once someone has bought something, no matter how small, she or he is now a customer, and this has real meaning.

Consistency and reliability are close cousins. "Reliable" is an adjective that is defined by the *New Oxford American Dictionary* as "consistently good in quality or performance; able to be trusted." In service, businesses strive for reliability in the form of consistency every day; it is the meat of their customer relationships. Inconsistency, on the other hand, is not trustworthy at all. Look up the word in the *Oxford American Writer's Thesaurus,* and you will understand why inconsistency is the bane of any business. "Erratic, unpredictable, inconstant, unstable, irregular, contradictory, paradoxical, fickle, mercurial [and] volatile" are words that are listed in this entry. This is a list of the worst possible words to describe any business, and these words explain why avoiding inconsistency is what you must strive for daily. Consistency is a habit, a good, reliable habit that demonstrates so much to our guests. But consistency must be built and maintained in order for it to work for us.

Jean François is the senior hair stylist at J. Sister's salon in New York City. Located on 57th Street just off Fifth Avenue, the salon is a small, high-end business that caters to many businesspeople in the Midtown area as well as to many high-profile clients. But the salon relies on its regular customers most of all. "Our regulars are our bread and butter," Jean François says; "a consistent experience is what keeps them coming back." What makes an experience consistent, he says, is treating each customer like an individual and listening to what he or she is seeking with that appointment. It also means offering more frequent little "tweaks" to customers' appearance rather than doing everything in one visit. These upkeep visits—a bang trim between haircuts, a neck trim for gentlemen, or a blow-dry once a week—are smaller sales that present great opportunities of providing service. "My best customers come more often but for the little things. And some clients have been coming to me for years even when they move out of the city or state. It is essential to evolve and grow with your customers, then they will stay with you," says Jean François.

This echoes Cialdini's point that these small commitments to a brand lead to the consistency of the customer over many years and turn customers into regulars. The trust has been built, the business has evolved with the customers, and this makes it easy for clients to commit to the salon and easy for the salon to retain valued customers. Another J. Sister's stylist, head colorist Michael, agrees and takes it a step further. "I try not to offer too many options to my clients. When they say they want something 'different' I will offer two options and act confidently in my choices. My customers respect me for it, and it keeps the decision-making to a minimum and limits stress." Michael makes the point that you must be confident in your job, and this inspires confidence in your customers. "If you don't drive the car, they will drive you around the block," he says, as too many choices are distracting and then create a daunting list of decisions to be made. Offering fewer decisions creates fewer distractions for customers and thus more confidence in you and your brand.

One regular client of the J. Sister's Salon, Jeffrey, has been getting his hair cut by Jean François for almost 20 years. The things that have kept him coming back are few: consistent service and the ability of Jean François to evolve along with his life. "When I met Jean François, he immediately addressed my troublesome areas and gave me a great cut. I always generally get the same cut, but through the years he always makes the cut look current. So each time I go I feel like he always makes me look my best." The glue of their relationship is that they have a strong professional bond. "Jean François always made me feel like I am a valued friend. I can call him anytime, and he will fit me in and he has always given me a great price. We have only gone out socially once or twice, but the feeling I have is more of 'friend' and less of 'client.' That means a lot."

Connecting with your guests is a small but valuable thing. Jean François says he keeps notes on his customers, noting their birthdays, family members' names, and recent changes (new home, kid's graduation). Michael says that remembering little important details about his clients ensures trust and when his clients trust him, he can do his job better because they are at ease. Building trust and delivering on that trust is essential to building a long-term customer relationship, a relationship that benefits both parties equally.

A Two-Way Street

It was easy to see how the large number of regulars at Balthazar was great for business, but after a few years I realized that the regulars were also good for the staff. When customers patronize a place regularly and get to know the staff, both the team and the customers feel good, are remembered, and at feel at ease. The regulars at Balthazar knew our names, remembered important things about our lives, and acknowledged our service around the holidays with gifts and tokens of appreciation. Being seen as a real person by these clients was so meaningful for the staff that it helped with retention. Turns out that the benefits of consistency apply to the staff as well.

Going to your job when you work as a barista, salesperson, or bank teller is vastly improved when you have a guest come in who knows you. When both parties are glad to see one another, it is beneficial to the professional relationship that they have forged. The customer wants to come back, and the staff member doesn't want to leave. Thus, consistency keeps your business vital as it connects people through habit and humanity. And like decency, humanity (remembering things about another person, being glad to see someone) has a power that is truly incredible.

Customers want the business they patronize and the staff they encounter to be reliable, stable, and informative. They want their salesperson or representative to offer informed choices, competitive rates, and proactive ideas that will provide quality and value for the money spent. When this happens, trust is ensured. Thus, you must ensure that your staff is knowledgeable and offers the same information to every guest so that each interaction is informative in a uniform way. No one wants to miss out on a better deal or a short window of opportunity when there is one available. Regular staff training is part of creating consistency, and this will do two things for your business. First, staff members will always have knowledge they can use to the best advantage of their customers and clients. Knowledge is power and this creates confidence in your team. Second, when your team can speak confidently about your products and with one voice, your customers will be able to trust the experience and the service that is being offered, no matter who is speaking to them. There is nothing worse for customers than to have questions go unanswered or to have doubt that the answer offered is correct.

Regardless of type of business you have, it is important to remember that you are not just delivering your goods, your brand, your product, but rather an experience for your guest or customer. Each moment (or "touchpoint") of the experience contributes to a positive association and then a positive memory. The time spent with your business has given your guest several experiences: the staff member or website, the timing of the experience, the quality of the experience, even the exchange of money (is it easy to process the order; is payment handled properly?), and finally the professional and friendly thank-you and good-bye. These are many moments; the guest has been impacted positively or negatively numerous times.

When all these moments are in alignment, you have given your guest the impression of "good service." The engine of the experience is humming and chugging along, and your guests are able to relax and enjoy the business. But when just one piece of the experience is missing, then the parts of the experience as a whole just don't add up. Instead, the experience has become inconsistent, and this dissonance creates dissatisfaction. One of my pet peeves is that when after a good dining experience—the food was good, the server was nice, the atmosphere was lovely—and after paying my bill, as I walk out the door nobody says good-bye. This leaves me with the impression that nobody noticed that my party and I are leaving. And this is enough to leave a patina of displeasure that now colors my memory of the entire experience.

Each time customers interact with your business, your staff, or your products, there is a possibility for a moment of service. These are the times when something can happen that makes a difference in your guests' experience. The change can come from any number of things—for example: a friendly hello or good-bye, assistance just when the customer wants it, a staff member remembering his customer's name, a problem that is swiftly corrected, being offered several options, and so on. What these moments of service do so well is create a memory for the guest. If the memory is great, then you have made a first-time guest into a regular or, at the least, the guest will have something positive to say to friends. If the memory is not so good, the first-timer may never come back, and the regular may not come as often anymore.

Our job is to offer our guests a consistent, trustworthy, and reliable experience that they can enjoy and take pride in. A business that can do this well will cultivate regulars. If you can do this well, you will cultivate people who are able to patronize your company and stand up for it. Your customers are a part of your marketing plan: their trust and belief in you helps to build your brand, one person at a time. This is not an advertising plan that trumpets news about your business to thousands of people at once; rather, it presents more of a grassroots approach. Your guests tell their friends, and they, in turn, tell others. Word of mouth is vital to your business being not only profitable but beloved.

Tips and Takeaways

- **Grow Regulars**. Develop your regulars by reaching out to the newest ones. In restaurants they have reservations systems that track their guests. It is natural to reach out to regular guests: they are familiar. The trick is to reach out to your new, first-time guests, one by one, and make contact. Engage them face-to-face or over the phone to create a moment of service that is meaningful and promotes a relationship.

- **Internal Consistency**. Consistency starts with the leaders in the business. How you address your staff, acknowledge internal issues, and solve problems for your teams is an aspect of consistency that affects your business. Your team notices everything you do, and everyone notices the way you lead. You must develop systems of working with the team so that you don't appear to be favoring one person or department over another or giving more attention to one group over another. Consistently managing your team will build trust in your leadership and decisions. You will be seen as a manager who is reliable and believable and consistent.

- **Build Loyalty**. Consider using innovative ways to promote the development of regular guests or creating a unique loyalty program. Loyalty programs can and should be easy to use and act as a bridge between your company culture and your guests. The culture piece is what makes your business memorable and interesting to your customers. They love to "peek behind the curtain" and see the inner workings of a business; you can share your business through your core values or company rituals. This makes it fun for your loyalists and creates intimacy through transparency. What are the core values and core interactions of your business? Capitalize on them to make an impact on your guests, an impact that will keep them visiting your business as often as possible.

- **Support Your Habit**. Consistency is a habit that can be built. In order to build the habit you must set a goal for the moments that must be kept consistent. Then develop an approach or a mind-set that gets you to your goal and involve people to support your idea. Involve your team and colleagues in your goal and ask for their support and commitment. Address the issue of consistency in meetings and one-on-one with your managers. Building a good habit takes time, but it pays off, every time.

CHAPTER 10

When Things Go Wrong

Say Cheese

"I wonder if they have a cheese sandwich." Nancy said to a group of friends while out for dinner at an Italian restaurant. Her husband Mark and their friend Andrew chuckled; they knew the story all too well. But the others at the table didn't get the reference so the three friends embarked on telling the cheese sandwich story. It went something like this:

A few years earlier, Andrew invited Mark and Nancy to spend the weekend at his home outside of Woodstock. Andrew's house is up on a hill surrounded by fields; there are few neighbors and fewer businesses. He often spends his weekends entertaining friends and family, walking his dog, and fishing in the nearby streams, lakes, and ponds. When Nancy and Mark arrived, they spent the morning outdoors enjoying the beautiful day, and then Andrew took them to a great deli in town to pick up some lunch.

The menu listed many hearty deli-style sandwiches in delicious combinations. Andrew and Mark perused the menu and immediately made their choices and placed their orders. Nancy, a vegetarian, didn't see anything on the menu that would accommodate her dietary preference; every sandwich contained some sort of meat. She asked the deli owner, who was working at the counter, if he could make her a cheese sandwich. He gruffly said he didn't have a cheese sandwich on the menu, despite the fact that the deli case contained a number of cheese options. Nancy persisted and asked politely if he could make her a cheese sandwich because she didn't eat meat, and he declined again. In desperation she then asked, "What if I order a turkey and cheese sandwich, and you leave off the turkey?" He got angry and with a raised voice indignantly exclaimed, "How am I supposed to price it?!" At this point the three friends looked at one another and unanimously turned around and walked out. His rigidity and inability to satisfy this simple request cost him more than the three sandwich orders that day. It also cost him a customer for life; Andrew has never returned.

In addition, the cheese sandwich story has become an oft-told tale that these three friends tell many times a year. This one little story retold by three different people is ultimately harmful for this business. The owner not only lost customers and missed out on cultivating a regular in Andrew, but the story lives on in dozens of people's minds. It is one of those service horror stories that spread like wildfire and become fodder for dinner parties and online forums for years to come. Two years later, the deli closed, no doubt in part because of a powerfully bad customer service story.

Little problems are actually big opportunities. I always say it's not the problem itself, it is how we solve the problem and make our guests happy that makes the difference. For example, I recently went to a restaurant and ordered a coffee with half-and-half. The server immediately said, "We don't have half-and-half; we only have milk—and cream," and was about to leave it at that. But she caught herself and made a quick correction: "So I can make some half-and-half for you, would that be okay?" And, of course, I said yes. This small correction made a small problem into a nonissue because she extended herself and thought about what I wanted and how she could fix it. This was a proactive decision that made a world of difference to my satisfaction in drinking that coffee.

When you are able to correct a problem in your business, no matter how small, you have created a memory for the customer about your brand. When problems aren't corrected, then the occurrence becomes a mental barrier that prevents a customer from returning and that becomes a story that is repeated to numerous people. Discovering the problems your customers are experiencing is a key element in the customer service equation and you must ask for feedback as much as possible. Jake Poore, a customer service expert who honed his skills working for nearly 20 years at the Walt Disney

Company, agrees that problems are an opportunity. He claims on his blog (Jake Poore Integrated Loyalty Systems) that up to 70 percent of customers leave your business without saying a word about their experience. He says, "If your customer goes home mad, it is not only too late, but they will tell their friends THEIR story. But if you can catch them and correct the error then they'll possibly tell YOUR story."[1] This is true; stories about service recovery are potent and can turn a poor memory of your business into a positive one.

In a press release on the AMEX website,[2] Jim Bush, executive vice president of World Service at AMEX says it all: "Getting service right is more than just a nice to do; it's a must do.... American consumers are willing to spend more with companies that provide outstanding service, and they will also tell, on average, twice as many people about bad service than they will about good service. Ultimately, great service can drive sales and customer loyalty." The American Express Global Customer Service Barometer, a study conducted by Ebiquity in 2014, explored the attitudes and preferences regarding customer service in the United States and nine other countries and determined that customers want a positive service experience more than ever.

The study showed that 78 percent of respondents said they have cancelled a transaction or not made an intended purchase when there was "subpar" service. Yet, 59 percent would try a new brand or business for improved service. In short, service matters. The report also showed that the service horror story is what people talk about most. Americans said that, on average, they tell 9 people about good service, but they tell 16 people about poor service experiences; that's nearly twice as many. Customers who said they had the best service experiences attribute this to friendly representatives who are able to correct any issues. Prompt, friendly problem solving; this is what people want in their customer service experience.

I maintain that most businesses strive to be good and even great, and this is what most customers expect. When an experience is good, this is simply meeting the customers' expectation; "good" is what the customer expects. Customers expect their service to be good so when it is good there is little to say (the good service meets my expectation). If the service is exceptional, then the customer may say more (the exceptional service exceeded my expectation), but if it is bad, the customer will certainly talk about that (the bad experience was much below my expectation). Bad service provides the opportunity for businesses to do more and better for their guests. And you must try to intervene while the guests are with you because bad service kills more sales than anything else.

Convergys is a customer management company that helps manage the customer service component for other businesses. The company offers phone-based customer service systems for its many clients in the fields of communication, cable and satellite, financial services, technology, health care, travel and hospitality, retail, and the automotive industry. Convergys operates in 31 countries, conducts customer service in 47 languages, and has experts in the field of solving problems for its clients' customers. In a study conducted by Convergys in 2014 called "U.S. Customer Scorecard Research: Key Findings on Customer Loyalty and Satisfaction,"[3] the company's researchers found that "the payoff for exceeding customer expectations is minimal compared to the penalty for not meeting expectations."

Regardless of type of business, when asked about their problem resolution experience, 66 percent of respondents in the study felt that their customer service expectations were being met, 22 percent felt that their expectations were being exceeded, and 12 percent felt their expectations were not met at all. But what is striking is that when asked how this affects future spending choices, those whose customer service expectations were exceeded were not more likely to spend more, with 16 percent reporting that they would actually spend less. In contrast, however, 61 percent of those whose expectations were *not* met when calling customer service said they would reduce their spending at the operations where the experience fell short. The damage happens when customer service expectations are not met, the basics are not being considered, and customers are left feeling unhappy and unsatisfied.

Convergys advises companies to eliminate "the top causes of dissatisfaction" with customer service. The biggest causes of dissatisfaction in problem resolution that they have monitored since 2009 are customers having to repeat themselves, having to contact the operation multiple times, and the resolution of the problem taking too long. To make people happy, it is essential that you take care of their needs first and foremost. When customers don't feel that the basics are being taken care of, then those moments designed to go "above and beyond" can fall flat. Customers who don't get this basic attention will leave your business with a bad memory, and this is damaging to your business and brand.

What this tells me is that you must meet customer expectations every time. You can attempt to exceed them only when the basics of service have been met. Too often companies are too focused on their own process and philosophy without considering the individual in front of them. You must first meet the customer's expectation by delivering a positive experience and product. You can then exceed expectations by engaging with your customers and offering options beyond what they had originally expected. Decency, in the form of meeting expectations, is at the heart of winning your customers. If more businesses would focus on delivering consistently and being swift and efficient in handling customers' problems, they would see a big improvement in their business and more loyal customers.

"Being amazing" doesn't make your customers happy as much as thoughtfully solving their issues and satisfying their requests in a timely manner. Demonstrating that you truly "put your guests first" by engaging and listening to them and then addressing their unique needs is what decency is all about. It is also what makes customers feel heard, considered, and respected as individuals. And this is where outstanding service shines: in all the little moments of consideration for your customers.

No Judgment

When talking to an upset guest, avoid saying no. "No" makes an impact that can almost feel like a slap in the face when a customer is asking for something. "No" transmits negativity and stubbornness, and it makes a big impression on our brains. In an article entitled "The Most Dangerous Word in the World"[4] published in *Psychology Today*, the authors, Mark Waldman and Andrew Newberg, write that "no" is a very dangerous word. In a study on the impact of "no," subjects were placed in an MRI machine, and those who heard or saw the word "no" for as little as one second demonstrated the release of dozens of stress-related hormones and neurotransmitters. The authors wrote that "these chemicals immediately interrupt the normal functioning of your brain, impairing logic, reason, language processing, and communication." In real life, when people express negativity by saying no combined with a slight furrowing of the brow, this negative effect on the other person is augmented. "The listener" they say, "will experience increased anxiety and irritability, thus undermining cooperation and trust."

This tells us how important your word choice is when speaking to customers, especially customers who are experiencing problems with your business. You must avoid using "no" whenever possible in order to retain the trust and cooperation your customers are showing your business and team. For example, I once worked with a manager named Michel who trained us on how to never say "no." His technique was called "yes, but." You never want to say "no" to your guests; however, sometimes it is impossible to say "yes." "Yes, but" is a way to accommodate guests' requests while also setting boundaries. For example, if your customer wants an item that you do not have in stock, rather than say you don't have it—the equivalent to "no"— you might say, "I can get that item for you, but it will take a week to get from our supplier. Shall I place the order for you?" Or you could say, "We no longer carry that item, but we have another that is very similar, and other customers have been pleased with it as a replacement." Giving boundaries to satisfying the request is key to satisfying the customer. If customers really want the product, they may decide to wait for it; if they don't want it that much, they may still remember that you made the effort to accommodate them.

In conducting service training for my clients I always share my seven basic rules for handling customer problems:

1. Always apologize
2. Never argue
3. Always give the customer the benefit of the doubt
4. Don't judge the information
5. Offer your help and/or get a supervisor
6. Remain supportive
7. Ensure the customer leaves happy

Of course, apologizing is the most important thing when your customers are not happy, but you must train your staff on how to offer an apology that is sincere. When doing staff training I always have participants role-play scenarios. For example, one person acts as the server, and one acts as the guest, and they are given a scenario to enact together, and then they switch roles. This allows each of them to take the role of the guest and give feedback to the person acting as a staff member. In this arena it is easier to practice saying "I'm sorry" and coming across as sincere.

"Never argue" is another point that needs to be articulated. Remember the medium rare steak? Many times the server will try to tell the guest that the steak is perfectly cooked, but this can be construed as an argument. You must train your team on standing up for the brand—but only up to a point. And if that point sounds like an argument, then it is time to be quiet and listen to what the guest has to say.

"Giving the benefit of the doubt" is a great way to demonstrate that you are on the customer's side. If a guest tells you that at his or her last visit things were "different," you don't want to argue the point or make a comment about that. The customer's point has validity and you must not doubt his or her experience when they go to the trouble of sharing their opinion with you. In response you might say "I'm sorry your experience is not the same; tell me what is different." The aim here is to get the customer talking without holding back because this information could be very important for that guest's experience and for the experience of other guests as well. And giving the benefit of the doubt will keep the communication open.

There are two parts to "don't judge the information." "No judgment" is a cousin to "giving the benefit of the doubt," and this is a skill you must train your staff to be aware of. Body language can show judgment just as easily as words; a downward tilt of the head says "seriously?" and a raised eyebrow says "no way" and rolling eyes tells guests you don't believe a word of what they are saying. "No judgment" is the backbone to "benefit of the doubt," and together these two mottoes are great for engaging a guest who is upset. I always tell my team that when someone is complaining or has a problem, that complaint "is just information." Don't react to it, don't take it personally, don't judge it; just take it in so the best solution can be found.

When staff members encounter an upset guest, they will get the supervisor or manager rather than try to handle the problem themselves. It is important to distinguish between getting your manager when things go wrong and trying to help the upset guest yourself. In step 5 above, "offer your help and/or get a supervisor," I like to empower staff members to help solve guests' problems, but I also like to set boundaries for what staff members are able to do for guests. For example, maybe staff members can make an exchange or refund guests' money up to a certain amount. Or maybe depending on the type of complaint, staff members can offer more loyalty points or offer something else for free. But when the stakes are higher—because the guest is very upset or the problem is unusual, for example—I recommend getting a supervisor or manager to assist with the solution. Accordingly, it is very important that you read your guests and the situation correctly. There are guests who will be reassured knowing that another person has been called over to assist; they think it demonstrates that their issue is being taken seriously. However, other guests will not want another person called over. Some are loath to be seen as a "complainer" or "don't want to make a big deal" out of their situation. In this case more people being alerted to their situation can make them feel worse, not better, about speaking up. Other guests will not want the manager to come if they feel they can get satisfaction from the person in front of them. But as manager or executive, you must make sure that your junior team members know they can ask for backup in assessing the situation. They should know that their ideas for a solution can be checked by a more experienced manager.

I have often found that when staff members have handled the problem and found a solution satisfactory to the guests, a manager or supervisor checking in on the guests can add value to the experience. However, this should be a light touch and a follow-up rather than a reopening of the case. I train teams to stay positive once the problem has been resolved as you don't want to remind guests of it if you screwed up; rather, you want them to remember that you made a great improvement. Often, after a problem has been solved and the guest is again happy, staff members acknowledge the problem once again as the guest is leaving; it is human nature to do this. Instead of "thanks so much, glad you enjoyed the dessert!" the server will remind the guest of the problem that was already solved by saying "have a good night and sorry, again, about the burnt steak." This brings back the old memory when the guest least wants to think of it.

Another key to service resolution is to "remain supportive." In many service scenarios when things go wrong, staff members want to run away; it is natural to want to avoid conflict. What you must train your employees to do is the opposite: they must remain close to the guests. For example, when a guest has a problem and is upset, staff members often stay away from that guest while the problem is being sorted out. This only gives the guest more to get upset about. Even the act of being put on hold can be infuriating. If the staff member in question is close by and remains supportive by sharing information that is helpful or by checking on the guest, the guest will not be ignored further and will be engaged in a meaningful way. Sometimes even making small talk can be a great distraction while the problem is being handled further up the chain of command. When an employee avoids the guest during a service recovery, there is no way to positively represent the brand. When your team member can engage the guest during these moments of downtime before the solution has been effected, the employee will be demonstrating confidence in the business by taking time to be with the upset guest. In addition, once the solution has been offered and accepted, the team member must stay positive and continue to engage the guest until the very last moment.

The last point is to make sure that your guest leaves happy. This seems obvious, but you must make sure by asking and finding out. Many people assume that a guest has left "happy," but until they have checked in with the guest, staff members have no way of knowing if happiness was achieved. They may have had one issue fixed only to have something go wrong again. Thus, it is essential to keep checking on your guests as long as they are with you or with your staff. As long as guests are engaged with your business, you can create a solution; when guests have left your business, this is much harder. The opportunity to wow your guests is there as long as they are with you; once they have left, that opportunity is gone.

Managers are quick to think that customers are only looking for a refund, and in some cases this is true. But I have found that when asking the guests what they would like the business to do, their answers are surprising. I have had guests who just wanted to "blow off steam," guests who wanted a favor to be done for their friend, such as giving them your card, and guests who wanted to "be right" and have their complaint acknowledged with sincerity. These are all small fixes that can be done in the moment. When a guest leaves without satisfaction, then you have squandered a moment to fix the situation. Once guests are home and dwelling on the problem, the stakes go up, and the opportunity for a "quick fix" has left the building with your guest.

Adding It Up

Luxury hotels are all about details. The way the bed is made, the way the toiletries are arranged on a vanity, and how the teacup is set on the table are all little details that tell guests they are in a luxury environment. Frequent guests of luxury hotels are accustomed to a high level of service, and the quality of the service is all about the littlest things. Igor Apraiz, a hotel manager with years of experience in the luxury market, knows that all the little details can add up to a great guest experience or to a lousy one. In the hotels he manages he trains his staff on how to see and acknowledge the smallest of errors and how to communicate them to others in the hotel. He calls these small issues a guest may have "glitches" and reporting them a "glitch report." "The best hotels in the world have the most glitches," he says. "Their managers have developed the best radar for seeing the smallest of issues, correcting them, and communicating these issues to their teams." Developing the "glitch radar" is part of the training, and all departments are responsible for seeing—and acting on—the glitches as they occur.

Guests have so many possible points of contact in a luxury hotel: in the room, the elevator, the bar, the dining room, fitness center, front desk, and front door. And there are just as many points of contact with staff members: housekeeping, host, waiter, maintenance, front desk, concierge, and doorman. These touchpoints can turn a guest experience from good into poor very quickly. A guest could wake up to cold water in the shower, then have issues with the Wi-Fi in the room, then have to call for a newspaper delivery that was already requested and, finally, go to the restaurant, get served coffee and the sugar caddy has only one packet of Splenda, but the guest needs two. Now, each glitch on its own can be construed as a "little" problem. But when the glitches add up, the result is a service nightmare for the guest.

The "glitch report" serves to record any and all guest issues and communicate them to the rest of the departments. This ensures that all hotel staff members are aware of the level of service that this guest is experiencing. Once a "glitch" is reported (either by the guest or by a staff member who has caught it), it is immediately written into a "glitch report" and forwarded to the front desk where it is entered into the guest's record. These records can be seen by anyone checking on this guest, and that staff person will know whether this is the first glitch or a glitch that is compounding others that preceded it. Then that staff member knows how to handle the service recovery.

If the problem (no hot water) is the only glitch, then a prompt solution and recovery is necessary with proper follow-up (sending a plumber to the room to fix the problem, offering another guest room for showering, and following up later in the day to make sure the problem was completely resolved). But if the glitch is no longer isolated and is now the most recent in a series of issues before noon, then the recovery may take a different tack. The Splenda issue, while seemingly very small on its own, may result in a complementary breakfast or a conversation with the guest about food and beverage preferences and then sending an amenity to the room. If the guest likes martinis, then a martini set—shaker, a preferred brand of vodka, olives, strainer, and martini glasses—will be placed in the guest's room to enjoy later that evening. When it comes to handling guest problems, it is imperative to stay ahead of the problem and be proactive on behalf of the guest—every time.

When training his team on how to handle a glitch, Apraiz goes through a series of steps with his teams. One of the most important aspects is to acknowledge the glitch, then respond with empathy, not commiseration. "There is a big difference," he says, "between the two." Empathy is feeling for your guest so when a guest tells you about having had to endure a cold shower, an empathetic response might be: "I'm so sorry to hear that, that is a tough way to start your day." Commiseration is joining the guest in the problem itself rather than showing empathy for the unique experience. "Oh no, you too? Everyone is calling about the cold water today, it's a mess!" Saying it is a mess involves the staff member and makes the problem into the staff member's own problem which reverses the roles. The person who must help is now in need of help him or herself. This does little to make the guest feel better, and it only makes things worse by implying that it is a bigger problem in the hotel.

"Instead of 'tolerating issues' you train your staff to see them and to handle them," adds Apraiz. And handling the little issues is really an expression of empathy toward your guests. You want to instill in your team a can-do attitude toward handling glitches. "I want my team to think 'how can I turn this guest around?' and use empathy to correct or improve a situation." Using empathy and acting on your guest's behalf is a great way to establish a bond and create a lasting relationship with your guest. Guests can trust you because you noticed the problem, and they felt cared for. With each glitch there is a moment of applying the principle "I notice = I care," and this can make a powerful and positive impact on guests and their experience of your service and your brand.

Tracking customer issues is helpful to your business and to your managers; it is a communication tool that improves the experience for both customers and staff. Having knowledge about customer problems allows your staff members to be proactive and confident in their approach with the client. Sharing knowledge allows the issue to be considered from other angles; do others share this issue, or can this problem offer an insight for innovation or improvement? Having an internal dialogue about customer problems and issues is the key to making your business better every day. This dialogue should include not only managers and supervisors but line staff as well because they are the ones who hear the most from your customers. They can offer insights and share common issues that customers face and even hear ideas from the customers themselves.

For example, something I loved about working at Balthazar was that our ideas for improvement were always valued. When the waiters all complained that the drinks were taking too long to come from the service bar and holding up the service to their guests, the management team decided to look at this issue. The issue was that there was an incredible volume of drinks that had to come from one tiny service bar area. With wines by the glass comprising 50 percent of the drinks served at the service bar, the solution quickly became clear: have the waiters serve and pour their own wines by the glass rather than wait for the service bartender to pour it for them. This required a renovation of the service bar, and an ice bin for the storage of white wine bottles was built on the side of the bar facing the servers. Additional shelves for the red wine bottles were added on the end of the service bar. This way the wines could be poured more quickly, and the servers were able to get back to their guests that much faster.

What I learned from working the front door of so many restaurants is that making corrections and offering solutions can really be quite easy. But it requires quick thinking combined with action. Moving guests to another table, offering a quick substitution when the food is not quite as expected, and sending a small item while the new dish is being prepared are all quick fixes that help correct a problem. In most businesses there are many options for making a guest happy. I always advise my clients' teams to "extend yourselves with excellent customer service." Extending yourself is about engaging the guests and following up when you are "reading" that they are not feeling great in the moment. This can be as simple as offering your name and offering your help and assistance. For example, "Hi, my name is Kate, is there anything I might help you with?" By following your instincts, checking in with your guests, and starting a conversation, you may find out more about the customers in front of you. And then you are able to offer a customer service experience that is focused on the guest. All staff members can extend themselves in this way and possibly help prevent more glitches from happening.

When things go wrong, little interventions can save the day. Connecting with the guest on a personal level, looking him or her in the eye, showing decency, and using active listening are all small ways that make people feel valued when expressing that a problem has occurred. In many businesses bad customer service can be alleviated even with little interventions. Often, little tokens of recognition are all that is needed to let customers know you acknowledge things went wrong, and you are trying to make them right.

Tips and Takeaways

- **Track Issues**. Problems are opportunities, but only when you use the problem to look at your business, your brand, and your staff and then make changes where necessary. Keep a running tab or log of the issues that are facing your customers so you can track issues that are plaguing your company. Not every complaint requires an overhaul of a product or service, so you must track the issues that come up, have dialogue with your team members, and make change only when necessary.

- **Get Comfortable**. Training and role-play are essential for helping your team members develop their skills in problem resolution. But don't just have them come up with scenarios and solutions on their own. Create roles and situations that help your teams develop skills regarding specific topics or scenarios. Offer those playing the role of "customer service rep" some options for service recovery so that they can practice proven methods for successfully helping a customer. This will help them improve their mode of communication and help them gain facility in addressing the issues your customers face.

- **Say Less**. Beware of giving too much context to your customers. Phrases, such as "it's her first day on the job," or "we just got this system installed," are begging forgiveness from your customer for the wrong reason. Why would you put someone so green in front of your customers or use a new system without training the staff or testing it first? Don't offer excuses; be proactive. Instead of "it's her first day," offer "I'm so glad Maria called me over to help you, let's see what I can do." It's a more proactive approach and doesn't throw Maria under the bus.

- **No Ego**. Beware of being too personal. When things go wrong in service, our team members are quick to share what made them make the mistake in the first place. "Sorry, I was up late last night with my new infant" may be the truth, but it puts the staff members' problems first rather than the customers'. Coach your team to offer a sincere apology and have confidence that an honest "I'm so sorry, I will fix that right away" is really what the customer is seeking in that moment.

CHAPTER 11

The Old-Fashioned Touch

The Power of a Handshake

Ask most people, and they will say they can tell something about a person by his or her handshake. This isn't just a fable but a true occurrence: people can tell something about a person by shaking his or her hand. The epitome of a good handshake is the "firm handshake"; it conveys something meaningful about the person you are meeting and paves the way for a good experience. But do people really still shake hands or is this an outdated convention? As it turns out, a handshake is something people are afraid of; because they're not sure how or when to offer it, they're afraid of making a bad impression. After all, when you receive a bad handshake, it can color your experience with the person you just met.

A study conducted by Chevrolet UK determined that 70 percent of Britons said they lacked confidence conducting this simple gesture: the handshake. As many as 19 percent of respondents reported "hating" handshaking because they didn't know how to do so properly. This study combined with low sales led the executives at Chevrolet UK to sponsor a study to see if they could improve the confidence and quality of handshakes in their sales team in order to boost sales. In the highly publicized study, researchers at the University of Manchester devised a formula for the perfect handshake. The formula combines many qualities: firmness, dryness, temperature, and grip—18 criteria in all—and Chevrolet conducted training based on this formula with its staff. Les Turton, sales manager for Chevrolet UK summed it up: "It is easy to overlook everyday rituals, but as the handshake is used to complete agreements, it is important our staff are well trained so they and can pass on trust and reassurance to our customers."

Chevrolet made an investment in an old-fashioned gesture. Chevy knows that this is not a mere gesture, but it is representative of the company and its brand. A handshake is a powerful gesture that can transmit a clear message about trust and reliability to your guests. Chevy made an impressive investment that we can all learn from when empowering our teams as they represent our brands, create an experience, and literally touch our guests.

The importance of a handshake is real, and neuroscience researchers recently proved this in a study entitled "The Power of a Handshake."[1] The study participants were monitored by an MRI and a machine that monitors sweat levels while they watched videos of people engaged in various business settings. When they saw videos where people shook hands, participants demonstrated a reaction that was like pleasure and lit up the area of the brain that processes reward, the nucleus accumbens. This is the same part of the brain that records our excitement for food, affection, and sex.

In an article about the study on the Beckman Institute's website author Steve McGaughey quotes the researchers as saying that "a handshake preceding social interaction enhanced the positive impact of approach and diminished the negative impact of avoidance behavior on the evaluation of social interaction."[2] That is, a handshake is seen as a positive, and it sets the stage for a good relationship while acting as a preventative to misunderstanding. One of the challenges facing service providers is often a simple misunderstanding between the staff and customers. A handshake can prevent these problems from happening at all. The researchers also found that the type of handshake was important. A firm, confident, and friendly handshake is the type that sends the positive message. In a study published in the *Journal of Personality and Social Psychology*[3] researchers proved that how you shake someone's hand can affect the impression the other person has of you.

In the study researchers trained four judges in the eight characteristics of a good handshake: completeness of grip, temperature, dryness, strength, duration, vigor, texture, and eye contact. These judges rated the handshakes of 112 participants, half of them male, half female. As part of the study, participants were invited to take a personality test and were welcomed to different parts of the test by various people (the handshake judges) who each shook the participants' hands. The results showed that across both platforms—the handshakes and the results of the written personality tests—those with a firm handshake had higher scores for positive and outgoing personalities than those with weaker handshakes, who demonstrated being more shy and anxious.

The study makes the case that a better, or firmer, handshake is important in making a good first impression. The first impression is especially important because of the halo effect (see chapter 3). The first impression serves to color the rest of the experience; therefore, if that handshake is firm, it sends a positive message not only about the person (trustworthy and outgoing) but also about the business the individual represents. This sets the stage for more positive impressions and starts the service experience on a positive note.

Your Mother Was Right

There is no romance when placing an order online. There is little interaction with the screen, and while the process is efficient, there is no way to touch our guests beyond delivering what they ask for. The opportunity to touch your guests more profoundly comes when they receive the item they ordered. Receiving a box in the mail can be a nice moment, the ritual of opening the box and pulling out the product conjures up images of Christmas morning, and this is a moment to capitalize on. When retailers send out that package to their guests, they have a great opportunity to add a little human touch. Including a handwritten note or some sort of personal recognition can have a big impact on your customers.

For example, Etsy, an online collective of artists and craftspeople selling millions of different handmade or artisanal items, sells anything from jewelry to candy to living room furniture, and each artisan has an online "shop" that is operated through the Etsy platform. In operation since 2005, Etsy has 1.4 million active sellers who have sold over $1.94 billion worth of inventory. The Etsy blog guides sellers toward getting the best results from their shops and offers helpful tips on how to attract clients who will love their brand.

In the section on the Etsy website entitled "Service Tips for Sellers: Packaging and Shipping," Etsy shares tips and ideas for sellers that will improve their customers' impression of them through little things like packaging materials and shipping methods. The website presents examples of what works and what fails and includes testimonials from customers to illuminate their points. Etsy advises sellers to "use your packaging to communicate with your customers. The little details count and can make your shop stand out and create an experience to be remembered."[4]

The folks at Etsy know that the experience of receiving the order is what makes one brand stand out above another in the customer's mind and that this is the moment to touch your guest: when your customer receives his or her package in the mail. They encourage their sellers to include a personal note, one that is hand-written or printed out. They explain that the note could be thankful or helpful and even suggest care instructions for the product purchased. They also advise using this moment to ask for feedback and include the following testimonial:

> I bought an item from an Etsy shop and opening it was like opening a gift. From inside a big bubble envelope, I pulled a bundle wrapped in tissue paper. It was tied with a ribbon and had a tag with my name on it. Instantly, my purchase felt much more like a gift. Inside was the item, nicely folded, a small gift in line with what the store sells, a business card, and a handwritten thank-you note.

Imagine now that you have also included a card that invites feedback? This is the customer you want to gain feedback from and his or her delight in the moment will inspire a glowing response either to you personally (include your e-mail address) or to the shop website (invite customers to leave a review on the site itself). You must remember that service is a conversation; when you invite your guests to connect with you, you should also take that moment to reach out with a thank-you and a request for feedback. This is something the people at Etsy understand and share with their online community.

Handwritten notes offer something more than a connection, a conversation, and gratitude. They offer permanence that no text message can replace. In an article on the *Harvard Business Review* website entitled "Handwritten Notes Are a Rare Commodity. They're Also More Important Than Ever," John Coleman states that handwritten notes have more meaning than an ordinary e-mail. "We don't print e-mails and display them on our desks, refrigerators, and mantles they way we do with letters and notes from friends. The physical notes are more memorable."[5]

He also explains that e-mails "are rarely notable. But handwritten notes are unusual. They take minutes (or hours) to draft, each word carefully chosen with no 'undo' or 'autocorrect' to fall back on. Drafting one involves selecting stationery, paying for stamps, and visiting a mailbox. They indicate investment, and that very costliness indicates value." The very action of writing and sending a handwritten note sends a message to your client—"I value you"—in the most straightforward way.

Coleman then quotes a November 11, 2011, *New York Times* article by John Tierney titled *A Serving of Gratitude May Save the Day* that says "an attitude of gratitude" has been linked to people being healthier, happier, and kinder than people who do not show their gratitude. That is, a thank-you note is a two-way street of kindness. It is a permanent way to impact your customer, and the act of writing and sharing the gratitude impacts the life of the writer as well. So yes, your mom was right, you must send out your thank-you cards after your birthday; this simple act has more of an effect than you would think!

One of the leaders in the notecard field is Hallmark. The company offers not only cards for any occasion but also "customer engagement" strategies for their corporate clients. On their website in the *Hallmark Business Connections Blog*, Hallmark offers ways for business people to send personalized e-cards to clients, and explains that business is about engagement with customers. The blog writers also distinguish different types of clients you may want to reach out to: first time clients ("newbies"), occasional customers ("casual buyers"), customers active on social media ("the social buzzers"), and former customers ("the lapsed customer"). You can touch each customer type with a note or e-mailed card. Hallmark maintains that sending out Hallmark cards can help continue, revive, or create a long-lasting relationship with your customers; according to the blog writers, "your customers want to feel good about being your customer." Connecting outside of the sale is a great way to continue the good feelings between your company and your customers.

Notes of any kind are wonderful for expressing gratitude but they also go a long way in apologizing when a product or experience falls short of expectations. The Hallmark website cites the "Customer Care Measurement & Consulting Customer Rage Study" conducted by the W. P. Carey School of Business at the University of Arizona. The study discovered that 62 percent of upset customers want an apology but only 38 percent receive one. And not any apology will do; a well-crafted apology is key to helping to turn an upset guest into one who feels considered and heard. It is essential for an apology to come across as sincere and to acknowledge the responsibility of the business for what went wrong; an apology should not ignore how the recipient feels.

For example, an article in *Psychology Today* entitled "The Five Ingredients of an Effective Apology," Guy Winch lists the five essential parts of a sincere apology:

1. A clear I'm sorry
2. An expression of regret
3. An acknowledgement that expectations were violated
4. A demonstration of empathy for feelings of the other person and the actions that led to those bad feelings
5. A request for forgiveness

Winch notes that empathy is the piece that is most commonly left out but is the most important. "In order for the other person to truly forgive us, they need to feel as though we 'get' the full implications of our actions," he says.[6] Expressing empathy can be difficult. Simple statements such as "I can imagine," "you must have felt...," or "I feel terrible for..." are all good ways to state that you realize how the other person must have felt. And this consideration, written out, is what has meaning for your customers.

Reaching Out Personally

At Highland Financial Advisors, Michael Gibney and his colleagues send out Thanksgiving cards rather than the requisite Christmas cards. They do this because many of their clients do not celebrate the Christmas holiday, and it is too easy for a card to become lost in the December holiday shuffle. It is important to Michael that his team takes time to thank the company's many clients personally. "We always mention how thankful we are that they show support and continued confidence in our company," he says. "Each advisor takes the time to handwrite a personal note to his clients then everyone else in the office signs the card as well. We start writing them in early October in order to finish by Thanksgiving."

Often clients respond with great feedback and share that they appreciate this personal touch from their financial planners. The key, Michael says, is to include a personal message that is not about finance. "We like to include a non-business related note like 'Go Giants!' or 'Enjoy the time with your son/daughter back for the first time from their freshman year of college', or 'I hope your mother/father is well.'" In order to keep up with these small acknowledgments, Michael and his colleagues keep notes on each of their clients in order to keep up to date with the client's personal interests or family. This sincerity is important in nurturing the relationships the advisors have with their clients, and it contributes to the success of the small company.

Highland Financial Advisors is not the only small company that depends on its customers' happiness. Rocco and Roxie is a small, family-owned company that conducts their business exclusively on Amazon. The owners are aware that they have limited ability to touch their customers, and they use thank-you e-mails as a way to connect with their customers firsthand. Rocco and Roxie sell a pet stain and odor eliminator. The product is one of the top in this category on Amazon, and the owners attribute their success to their great product, their 100-percent money-back guarantee, and very satisfied customers. Paul, one of the owners, explains that they "want to give their customers a warm and fuzzy experience with the brand." From the moment the company started receiving orders, the owners decided to acknowledge every order with a personal e-mail of thanks.

This has created quite a stir. Every few days they receive a reply from customers that says "Wow, I didn't expect that." Their customers commonly write back not only to acknowledge that they like the product but also to acknowledge that they love the "old-fashioned touch" of receiving a thank-you note via e-mail. In the e-mail Paul thanks his customer for purchasing the company's product and says they're "a small, family-run business committed to giving you a 5-Star experience." One recipient even wrote back to ask "are you really a small family business?" thinking that this was some giant company trying to establish a small-business vibe. Paul called the customer, introduced himself, and said that his company is indeed a small business—much to the client's surprise and delight.

In the e-mail Paul also lets his customers know that he personally will answer all e-mails and offers them an 800 number if they prefer to reach him by phone. He also makes a simple request: if his customers are happy with the product, he would like them to post a positive review on the Amazon site. Paul maintains that these e-mails (he sends one when the order is placed and another one a week later to check how customers like the product) are the key to the company's success. And the proof is online where almost two thousand customers have left positive reviews in praise of the company, its product, and its impressive customer service. The time it takes to send an e-mail and a personal response is small in relation to the positive response elicited from customers; the e-mails to customers have helped build Rocco and Roxie into a profitable small business intent on growing its product line even more.

Paul is aware that online the reviews are what counts, and engaging his clients by e-mail or phone is key to connecting with them and making sure they are satisfied. When a customer isn't happy, the company always refunds the person's money in full and thanks the customer for the feedback and patronage. This connection goes a long way toward promoting the company's brand, a brand that is not sold in stores. Moreover, the company's customer service gives a face and personality to its online store. The old-fashioned connection is the key in making this online company human and trustworthy to their legions of loyal customers.

Courting in the Computer Age

Sirio Maccioni is a restaurant legend. His career blossomed at some of the great restaurants in New York City in the 1960s, and then in 1974 he opened Le Cirque—"the circus" in French—in Manhattan. It became an immediate hit and set the bar for incredible food, wine, and service in the restaurant world. Sirio has been regarded as one of the best in the business and has developed a reputation as an incredibly hospitable host; now in his eighties, he still works in the restaurant to this day. Throughout his career, Sirio met hundreds of thousands of people in his restaurants. One of the skills he developed was the ability to recognize his many guests by the sound of their voices—and this was before the days of caller ID. Sirio has a profound auditory memory and knew who was on the other end of the line before that person said his or her name—much to the caller's delight.

Through the years as the restaurant took on more technological advances, Sirio was hard to impress. He hated modern conveniences, such as the POS computer system and phones with caller ID. The very notion of caller ID was ridiculous to Sirio. "You should know the sound of your guest's voice," he would implore the hosts and maître d'. "You don't need the number to tell you who you are speaking with." The computer systems were just as meaningless to him because they are often positioned so that the server faces the computer to input an order and thus faces the wall. "You must never turn your back on your guests," he would say, dismayed each time a server turned his or her back on his or her section to input an order to the kitchen.

These seemingly old-fashioned notions are very pertinent. How your staff interacts with technology can be a good thing (it does improve efficiency), but you must be aware that there can be a trade-off. Using technology cannot replace the human experience; you must focus on human contact and personal interaction as part of your service. One thing that Sirio misses is using the telephone. It has largely been replaced by computerized reservation systems. "The beauty of speaking on the phone is that you have a chance to interact with your guest and understand his feelings and emotions before he even arrives to your business," he shares. You can discover a lot of information over the phone by interacting and asking questions in order to better understand the guest's expectations for the dining experience. You also have the chance to assess how the guest sounds and might be feeling while you are interacting.

When guests arrives at the door, rather than refer to the computerized reservation system, which is at waist height at the host desk, Sirio asks his hosts to memorize the guests' names in order to connect with their guests when they first arrive. "You must make—and keep—eye contact with your guests when they enter the restaurant," he says. "If you have memorized your guest's name, when he arrives and tells you his name, you can keep the connection with this guest by looking in his eye and saying 'we're glad to see you, Mr. Jones, we were expecting you,' which helps the guest feel important." This demonstrates your respect in a way that looking at a screen does not. When you look away, you break the connection and lose out on a very human moment of contact.

Sometimes Sirio makes calls to his guests to say "I miss you, you must come back to the restaurant," and this makes a big difference to his clients. "People go to what's new rather than what's good," he says, so they need a reminder that your business is still there. And this personal moment tells guests that they are important to you and to your business. Especially now that most communication is by e-mail, a phone call with a personal message bears additional weight and meaning. This is something Sirio calls "courting your guest." Courting your guest is just as it sounds: creating a relationship, moment by moment, that allows the guest to put his or her trust in you and believe in your sincerity. Not unlike dating, courting your guests has a touch of romance in that it is about face-to-face communication, eye contact, using your senses, and creating an experience that considers your guests and makes them feel special.

Using your senses is a key part of building a relationship with your guests. The way things feel, smell, look, sound, and taste trump every image on a computer screen, no matter how beautiful those images are. You must consider how to involve the senses of your guests when the experience at hand is two-dimensional—an e-mail, written signage, or a computer screen. Sirio implores his captains to "tell people about the menu as if you were telling them a poem or describing a work of art." This is a way to create a picture of the food and helps to include another sense (what things taste like) when the guests are currently limited using only sight when reading the menu.

You also need to be concerned about the guest experience once they have left the business; you have helped them create memories of your business while they were with you, but when they have left, it is hard to make the experience come alive again. At Le Cirque the captains give a little gift to guests as they are departing in order for the guests to continue the experience at home. The captains are overt about this message, and as they give the chocolates to the ladies at the table, they say "this is something for you to remember us by." There are many little tokens or giveaways that you can give your guests: a pen, key chain, or notepad are all small items to keep the positive experience in the front of your guest's mind. It is imperative to make the connection between the item and what your hopes are. By telling your guests to "remember you" when you give them a token, you are continuing the courtship and reminding them positively of your business.

"It's hard to express authenticity, tradition, and charm through a computer screen" says Sirio; yet, that is our challenge in social media. Sirio makes the distinction between the limited remote experience (on a screen) versus the lush in-person experience. "You cannot truly express yourself in two dimensions; feelings and emotions are completely limited on a screen." He explains that there are three moments in the guest experience: pre-experience, the experience itself, and post-experience. The pre-experience, which is generally online, is two-dimensional and is limited to the facts and a description of what is to come. The actual experience is three-dimensional; this is where the feelings and emotions are expressed and felt and where all the senses are engaged. Post-experience there is a combination of 2-D (facts and descriptions) and 3-D (facts and experiences plus feelings and sensations). The pictures and comments your guests post online are 2-D, but the firsthand story can convey the feelings and sensations they experienced firsthand in the restaurant. And post-experience they are doing the work for you based on their positive 3-D experience. "Your guests are your social media managers," Sirio says; their experience is more important than ever.

On the holidays the restaurant upholds another time-honored tradition: sending out hundreds of hand-written holiday cards to guests and vendors.

But for a few select guests the managers go one step further and give them a Bûche de Noël (a Yule log), a traditional French holiday cake that is baked on the premises and is the epitome of holiday charm and deliciousness. The cakes are made fresh in the restaurant and then are packaged for delivery. This is not a job for FedEx or a courier; the family delivers these thoughtful gifts personally to their recipients' homes, just days before Christmas. "It continues the romance of the food and experience and allows us to personally touch our guests at the holidays." This is something no computer can compete with. "Bringing food to your guest's home is a way to strike the senses that cannot be touched by computer or e-mail." Many businesses send out food gifts at the holidays; if there is a way to make that moment more personal by delivering the gift yourself, you have just truly courted your guest in a memorable and thoughtful way. In Sirio's words, "certain things are irreplaceable," and your presence and efforts will not go unnoticed.

Tips and Takeaways

- **Test Their Skills**. Do some hands-on training with the members of your team who interact directly with customers, and do a handshaking workshop. Break your team into duos and have them evaluate the other's handshake based on the eight criteria of a good handshake. This allows team members to practice and confront a potential fear when meeting customers for the first time. It also allows your teams to engage with one another and use their skills of empathy while they report feedback to their colleagues. They can each sit in the seat of the guest and consider how their actions affect others—all in the safety of an internal training session.
- **Send a Card**. Consider sending holiday cards to your customers and clients. You may find a unique holiday to celebrate. If you have a kid-oriented business, send out Mother's Day cards; if you produce your goods in the United States send out a Fourth of July card; get creative with your holiday outreach and take a moment to sign the cards personally.

- **Tacit Connection.** Consider ways to engage your customers' senses, when they are with you or after they have left. A note elicits the sense of touch, a gift of food or drink inspires the taste buds, a phone call connects you to your client by sound, a video conference utilizes sight and sound, and sending flowers can fill your clients' offices with an amazing scent.
- **Take Notes.** Take notes so you can remember something personal about your clients or customers when you see them or reach out to them. Sharing an important memory of them (knowing their name, remembering their children, or knowing their favorite sports team) makes your call, card, or greeting that much more sincere and demonstrates that they are unique and special to you.

CHAPTER 12

Don't Scratch That Itch

Self-control

Ben and Ramona got married in 2004 and never took a honeymoon. They always said they would do it when they had more time and money, but then ten years passed and they still hadn't made time for a romantic getaway. One thing they had been doing was adding money to a honeymoon fund, and in 2014 they realized they had put away enough for a nice trip; it could be even nicer if they booked off-season at an upscale resort. One night Ramona was surfing the Internet and found a fantastic deal: book five nights and get two nights free at a Caribbean resort anytime between May and October. Considering their budget and their upcoming anniversary in June, they booked the hotel and got their airline tickets.

They arrived at the warm airport and headed to the rental car desk located just down the hall from the baggage carousel. The rental car check-in was some distance from where they were in the terminal, and as it was off-season, this area was quite empty. There was no line of customers and as they approached the various rental car area they could clearly identify the agents for each company at the continuous reception desk. As they got closer the agent from their company looked up, smiled and appeared ready to help. But the agent at the next company was clearly daydreaming. Her head was cocked at an angle, and she was dreamily in her own world. She was also biting her fingernails with some ferocity, and clearly not aware that anyone was looking. Ramona and Ben looked at each other quizzically, and then turned their attention to the agent in front of them who raised her voice with a warm greeting. This knocked the other agent out of her daze: she raised her head, lowered her hand, and assumed a more professional pose. From then on Ramona and Ben referred to the other rental car agent as "the biter." This became their running joke for the rest of their stay and is an anecdote they recount as a colorful part of their honeymoon story.

But this is not just an example of public grooming habits. This is an example of self-control. In every business the staff and managers must exhibit extreme amounts of self-control whenever they are in "guest-facing" areas. Self-control (controlling human urges) is essential to service as it contributes to two essential parts of the customer experience: trust and communication. Trust is a key piece of the service interaction. Customers routinely trust that everything in a business is going to be sanitary and working properly. When staff members forget about self-control (coughing into their hand then touching merchandise), then the trust that your guests walk in with can be broken. Self-control is a key aspect of communication as well; your body language speaks volumes about what you are thinking when in front of your customers. If you are slouching rather than standing straight, you have just communicated "lazy" or "disinterested" rather than "ready and waiting to serve." Self-control allows you to communicate the right things and represent your business properly.

You must always be aware of yourself. You must be mindful that your actions send very powerful messages to anyone who might be watching. Your customers take mental "snapshots" of your business. When they observe a staff member smiling and engaging with a guest, that becomes a snapshot and then a memory of the smiling service experience. But people will take mental snapshots of not so great moments as well: the staff member crouching behind a counter in order to read an e-mail on a smartphone or the supervisor rolling his or her eyes as a guest passes by. These become memories that stick in your customers' minds and that influence the experience they have with your business.

Manners and etiquette both depend on self-control in a social setting. I recently visited my college town in New England, and my husband and

I chose to spend the night in a stately old hotel in the center of town. The hotel has been in existence since the early 1900's and is kept in a very classic style: fireplaces, long drapes, and framed letters and memorabilia from the old days. One framed item was a sign from the turn of the century that asked ladies and gentlemen to refrain from spitting in public. This sign once was a common sight in many fancy and upscale environments. These days we take for granted that people no longer do certain things in public, and spitting has fortunately fallen out of fashion. Back in the old days people needed a sign to remind them of public courtesies, and now it is taken for granted that most adults will exhibit some form of social self-control when in public. We assume that most people have manners and will restrain their physical urges; even innocent sneezing, while necessary and sometimes quite unstoppable, is often accompanied by the requisite "excuse me."

Self-control is linked closely to professionalism. People at the top of their profession in any field demonstrate great amounts of self-control, whether it is controlling their emotions, actions, or words. Especially in our world now, everything is monitored and captured by various types of devices (cameras, phones, recording apps) and then shared and blasted through our homes via the media (Internet, TV, and print). To be at the top of your game requires great self-control. Top executives regularly seek assistance from executive coaches who offer advice on how to speak to staff and the media and how to "lead by example." Leading by example is a key aspect to service because it demonstrates the desired impression the lead executive or manager wants to impart to his or her team and then to customers and clients. Professionalism, as vague as this word is, really is the guide for most businesses. Essentially, professionalism means "not amateur," and this is how most businesses seek to be viewed.

By asking your team to exhibit self-control and professionalism, you are asking them to embody the highest ideals and actions of the top managers in order for the business to be seen as professional, viable, and trustworthy. People will spend their money in lots of places as long as they trust that they are getting their money's worth. Professionalism is as simple as acting in the best interests of the business by putting your own needs second to the needs of the business and its customers. Managers who demonstrate professionalism are important to the entire business because their self-control sends a strong message to the rest of the team.

For a paper published in the *Personality and Social Psychology Bulletin* and entitled "Regulatory Accessibility and Social Influences on State Self-Control," researchers conducted five different studies that proved that self-control, or the lack thereof, can be contagious. People take cues from those around them that are so powerful that they will either demonstrate more self-control themselves or ignore their own inner compass when around—or even thinking of—people who are not controlling their own impulses.

The study revealed that merely thinking of a friend or person who exhibits self-control (exercising regularly, for instance) can make a person's own self-control improve. On the other hand, thinking of someone you know who exhibits poor self-control (someone who drinks too much, for example), even for a second, can make your own self-control wane and grow weak in these moments. The lead author of the study, Michelle van Dellen, says that the study demonstrates that "by exhibiting self-control you're helping others do the same."[1]

Once you understand that self-control is a group behavior, you can see how your teams work and how they impact your guests. If your managers or lead staff members are exhibiting more self-control and professionalism, then the rest of the group will be more likely to do the same. And, of course, if just one person is showing a lack of professional poise, then the rest of the team will be more likely to join in and slack off. This can greatly impact the customer service experience. We've all had an experience of needing help in a business and watching as a group of team members collects in a corner talking among themselves while we are left watching their unprofessional behavior. This also shows how important your supervisors and managers are to setting the tone of our business. When a manager loosens his or her professionalism or personal poise, this can greatly impact the team and then the customer's impression of the business and of service. Self-control is a key aspect of the customer service experience.

Self-control, or the ability to control oneself in public, can have a big impact on any business. Because your employees represent your brand, it becomes essential that they demonstrate self-control and have an awareness of how they appear to others. Especially when those others are valued or potential clients it is of the utmost importance how their behavior is perceived. Businesses regularly retain executive coaches to help groom their top managers to help them improve their leadership skills or interpersonal skills. And sometimes coaches are brought on board to help managers better understand how their behavior is impacting their career and their clients.

When it came time for a top technology research firm to hire its next CIO (chief information officer), the executives had a difficult decision to make: hire from outside the company or promote one of their most talented IT managers, who lacked self-awareness. Ellen was a smart and obvious candidate for the role of CIO However, her lack of professional demeanor was causing her managers to doubt her ability to take on this more public role in the company. Before making a final decision, the company decided to bring in an executive coach to help Ellen improve her chances at taking this role, and Cynthia, an experienced executive coach, was chosen to work with her. The company leaders had briefed Cynthia that Ellen was brilliant but had no professional poise, didn't dress the part, and was very casual in the language she used in the office. While these traits were starting to affect how Ellen was perceived in the company, the executives were especially concerned about how Ellen would represent their brand to their clients. They were worried that her words and presentation could potentially come across as insulting. "The actions and behaviors that people first see undermine Ellen's enormous talent," Cynthia shared.

Cynthia met Ellen, and the latter's appearance was not in keeping with a top executive and in addition she showed a lack of awareness of her facial expressions; she was quick to show annoyance, irritation, and exasperation as a commentary on any topic of conversation. Moreover, she used very casual language and often made inappropriate jokes with those around her, punctuating her jokes with curse words. But Ellen did have an awareness that this could be damaging to her career, and in her first session with Cynthia she said that she wanted to work on her executive presence. The opportunity to become CIO—a female CIO in the male-dominated tech world—was enough to inspire Ellen to check her behavior in order to be seen as a contender for the role of a lifetime.

Cynthia's goal was to help Ellen find a role model of a woman in charge that felt authentic to her. She gave her a book called *Executive Presence* by Sylvia Ann Hewlett and they talked through the three pillars of executive presence—how you act, how you speak, how you look—all points that got Ellen's attention.[2] Cynthia also recommended a number of TED talks with female speakers for Ellen to watch and analyze: what were they doing? How did they project executive presence? How were they speaking to the audience? And how did they hold themselves so that they held their audience's attention? All good examples for Ellen to see, identify, and then apply to her own style.

Because Ellen was so expressive in her facial expressions, Cynthia also worked to help Ellen identify her personal triggers when she was speaking with her reports, with a client, or with a superior. Cynthia had her use a mirror when she was talking on the phone and for practicing in their sessions. This awareness was very helpful as Ellen then had knowledge of what made her react and how this was expressed in her face. She had not known that seemingly small gestures made such a big impression on those she was speaking to. And by finding a way to anticipate her own reactions to various situations and her personal triggers she gained a power over herself that also added to her confidence.

Finally, Cynthia made a video of Ellen doing a presentation so that she could see for herself how her actions speak for her and how much progress she had made. The video was an undeniable impression of how Ellen presented herself, and she immediately identified a number of areas to work on. The way she held her arms, tilted her head, rolled her eyes, and avoided looking at the camera gave the impression of someone not comfortable in her role. Ellen used the video as inspiration and by the end of her work with Cynthia she had improved her confidence in her body language and facial expressions. Ellen, in the end, was offered the job, and her reaction was genuine: happy, honored, and excited to move up the ladder. And her superiors felt much more confident in Ellen as she had taken time to learn and apply the tools needed in order to project the role she was meant to fill. Lead the business with confidence and poise.

Trust Me

Trust is the unspoken but obvious currency in any business transaction. Customers routinely trust businesses to do what they say, be respectful of their privacy, show care with their payments and credit cards, be fair with pricing and quality, and be reliable. Trust is a huge part of making sales in any business, and these actions will inspire our customers' deeper trust or will chip away at the trust that was already given. It is important to be aware that your customers notice your employees because the latter are standing in a particular spot, sitting at a desk, or wearing a uniform or nametag. This makes the staff more apparent to the guests. This is intentional and is a professional choice created to identify the staff to the customers. But this means that the actions and words your staff uses are on display and will be noticed by your customers. And what they notice will either support or dissipate their feeling of trust in your business. Therefore, you must try to eliminate any moments of doubt in the guests' experience of your business. You must uphold and value the trust your guests put in you at every turn.

Self-control is a huge part of communicating trust. Body language counts far more than actual words in most face-to-face communication (93% of communication is said to be nonverbal), and thus self-control is essential when speaking to strangers. The way you stand, gesture, react, and respond indicates your thoughts and can either support your words or undermine them. Self-control when speaking is a skill that must be taught and reinforced—day in, day out—in any business where there is face-to-face interaction with customers. A slouch shows disinterest, looking away appears distracted, hand on a hip appears indignant, crossed arms send a message of "don't bother me."

But it is not just nonverbal aspects of language that make an impact; how you say things is just as important. As introduced in chapter 1, para-language, or vocal communication, is the intonation of your voice and the emphasis you place on certain syllables. It is a key element of communication as it colors the words you are using. Vocal inflections make clear the difference between an enthusiastic "yes!" and a weary "yes." You must be aware of how you enhance your language with vocal inflections as these stick in your customers' minds and impact their overall experience. I always remind the staff members I train that they will be watched by their customers so they must exhibit self-awareness in what they do and how they speak. This self-awareness is a full-time job, and those who do it well make a positive impression on their clients. Understanding that you and your actions contribute greatly to the guests' experience gives you power: power to enhance the trusting relationship and power to positively impact your guests' experience.

Many executives understand the power that their actions and presentation may have on their clients. For example, Nora, an executive in the media industry, retained a personal shopper when she made the transition from advertising manager of *People* magazine to publisher of *Life*. Nora wanted to upgrade her wardrobe in order to fill this position and "send the message that I was in a new role." She went to Bergdorf Goodman and met Judith, an experienced personal shopper. Judith made a great first impression; she was perfectly dressed and had a calm and confident way of speaking with Nora that immediately made her feel at ease. And feeling at ease was top on Nora's list as she found choosing a personal shopper quite stressful. "You are entrusting your appearance to a stranger and will spend time in a dressing room together so I had to feel comfortable with my choice" she said. Judith's professional poise, calm demeanor and tone of voice were key to Nora feeling good about the first meeting.

Judith was also very good about making choices for Nora that fulfilled Nora's specific needs and weren't about the commission. A personal shopper makes a commission on what she sells to her clients, and Nora fully expected that Judith would do the same. However, Judith had a different approach. When Nora was invited to attend an event with Princess Diana, she had to find a ball gown for her appearance at this important gala. This was no average dress: it would serve as a visual message that would represent both Nora and her company. She wanted to find something that expressed her own personal style while matching the level of position she now held; the gown had to demonstrate her position and personality.

With formal gowns costing many thousands of dollars, Nora was expecting a huge investment for a dress she would likely wear only once. When she met Judith at the store to try on the gowns the latter had pulled for the event,

Nora put on a number of stunning dresses that were all beautiful, but none was a knockout. Judith pulled out the last dress and said, "I think this is the one" in her calm voice and with a confident nod of her head. Nora tried it on, and it was the winner: it was elegant, structured, and understated.

But Judith shared even more. "I remembered that you had this event coming up and I saw this dress on the clearance rack. I grabbed it for you and put it deep in the storage area hoping no one would put it back on the sales floor." Judith had selected the perfect dress for Nora that also happened to be a fraction of the cost of the other gowns on display. Her confidence in her choice and her conscientiousness for Nora's budget gave Nora both a perfect gown and confidence in her shopper. Judith was truly on her side and her actions and tone inspired the trust that Nora was seeking to place in this close advisor. Judith also helped Nora achieve her goal by making her outward appearance match the level of her new job. These wardrobe choices helped Nora represent herself and her business as classy, confident, and incredibly poised; both to her clients and, on one occasion, to royalty.

Don't Lose Control

Self-control is especially important in helping out with an upset customer. Your demeanor can help improve a situation or actually cause it to get worse. In his book *If It Weren't for the Customers I'd Really Like My Job,* author and psychologist Robert Bacal writes that the "first step to improve your self-control is to identify the triggering behavior that gets to you."[3] Triggers are those "hot buttons" that get to all of us and include tone of voice (yelling, patronizing), actions (pointing, touching), content of comments (racist, sexist), and even certain words. Once you become aware of the things that trigger you to lose control, then you will be that much more able to use your self-control when dealing with a difficult and upset guest.

As the book explains, even having a list of "self-talk strategies" can help you maintain your poise and self-control when someone is being belligerent or aggressive. If "you can remind yourself that this person is angry at the situation, not you, or remind yourself that this person has a right to be angry, you are more likely to maintain self-control," writes Bacal.[4] Thinking of phrases like "this person really needs some help" or "I can handle this" or even "they must look funny naked" helps to keep our triggers at bay and our poise and professionalism in the driver's seat. Self-talk is a proven way to exhibit and maintain self-control; Bacal writes, "Change your self-talk, and you can be more calm and effective." This is a great solution for both clients and staff members.

Bacal also makes the distinction between aggressive and assertive behavior. When you are dealing with an aggressive customer, you may be tempted to respond with equal amounts of aggression. In customer service you cannot fight fire with fire, but you can demonstrate assertive behavior in those moments rather than aggression. Assertive behavior is expressed by talking "calmly but firmly, if necessary. It also means that your physical posture must be confident rather than too passive or aggressive."[5] Assertive positive actions rely on a modicum of self-control, and this is the key to defusing a potentially aggressive interaction with a guest.

Another way to respond to aggression is with passivity. Bacal describes the impact of passive behavior in another of his books, the *Defusing Hostile Customers Workbook*:[6] "Some people believe that the more passive you are, the less likely people are to be nasty to you. The problem with this is that passivity will entice a bully to redouble their efforts at intimidation. They will sense your discomfort, and continue to attack if they feel you are off balance or weak." You must train your staff about self-awareness so that you develop a team of assertive, confident professionals who are guest-oriented and are neither passive nor aggressive. Engaging your team regarding possible difficult customer interactions, conducting role play in order for staff members to practice in a safe environment, and taking time to give feedback when a real situation has occurred can help your staff develop stronger self-awareness that will improve and positively impact your business in the long run.

Control What Is Controllable

When I was a restaurant manager, my job was to manipulate the image that guests take with them by working with staff members and reminding them to demonstrate and utilize self-control. During service I would start my rounds at the host desk and ask the hostess not to lean on the host stand (looks weary: the opposite of ready); then I would ask the bar servers to straighten out the stack of trays and organize the supplies that were used at the computer station (don't want anyone to think "unorganized mess"). Then I would ask the server to adjust his tie so that it looked crisp and ask another server to retie her apron strings so that they looked neat and fresh (halfway through the shift the staff should still look "fresh and ready for our guests" no matter the hour). Then I would take a look at the bar, asking for the garnish trays to be refilled and the glasses to be restocked (we don't want to appear like we've been through the ringer after the pre-theater rush). Then I would move on to the stations where I would send the busser to the bathroom to wash his hands after picking up a glass by the rim (that's unhygienic). And I would remind the server with the long ponytail not to adjust her hair in the middle of the dining room and then send her to the bathroom for an adjustment and hand washing (don't want anyone to wonder if her hair will land in the food). This would go on and on, from giving a server a mint after a smoke break to asking another server to flip his apron so it would look more fresh than the other side (and chefs too: they can button their chef's jacket on either the right or left side which serves to cover up the understandable stains that are part of the job).

Part of the job of the manager is to control what is controllable each moment of service. This is a clear visual message to the customers as well, as they see everything including subtle and caring corrections. Managers uphold and control the image of their business by controlling their actions and asking the staff to exhibit self-control at all times. These little images contribute to the big picture that guests take with them. They contribute to the memory guests are creating while in our business and will influence their decision to come back again.

Self-control is an essential piece of the training puzzle because self-control is linked so closely to professionalism. Professionalism means acting in the best interests of the business by putting the needs of the business and its customers first. Thereby, if customers are rude and unreasonable, you may be irritated by their behavior but you must fight your desire to tell them off because that will color their impression—and that of bystanders—of your business. You can't take back an impression.

Therefore, you must train self-control. You must train your staff members to notice how powerful their actions and words can be. You must give them examples and demonstrate options that will help them represent your business the way you want them to. You must also be humble and look at yourself first. If you, the leader or manager of your business, are letting your self-control slip, this is giving everyone on the team a reason to relax self-control as well. I see many managers failing to uphold the brand when they use their cell phone on the sales floor, choose to wear an outfit that is not in keeping with the uniform guidelines, or fraternize with staff members in a relaxed and careless manner. This reflects poorly on you but it creates an indelible impression in your guests' minds that impairs their trust in you and in your business. You must uphold trust with every word you utter and every action you take. It is essential.

Tips and Takeaways

What are the areas where you and your team must demonstrate self-control? Think about your actions and words as social graces that must be trained and practiced and discussed with your teams.

- **Talk it Out.** Conduct one-on-one feedback sessions with your managers and supervisors about their professional poise. Invite them to give you feedback as well about various aspects of your professionalism that impact them. This dialog is essential in learning more about oneself while upholding the standards for managers in your business. It also includes you in the conversation and allows you to improve your awareness of your professional poise, allowing you to "walk the walk" with confidence.
- **Training Happens Daily.** Consider the aspects of your business that are controllable and address them every single day. Share the concepts that most need work with your management team and create a task force to address all the little pieces of your business that are affecting your guests. Invite the team to "control the controllable" in their own areas on their shifts and ask them for feedback on what they were able to impact each day.

- **Check It Off.** Create a checklist for managers when they open and close the shop so they can make sure everything is presentable to the guests every day. This helps maintain standards, but it is also a method of communication back to you about your business. Make sure that any troublesome areas are being addressed and monitored to ensure positive results and an evolving and successful business.
- **Embody Professionalism.** On your feedback forms ask your clients about their impressions of your business and their impressions of your team. "Was your customer care operator open and helpful?" or "Tell us how our managers made an effort to impress you today" are both great open-ended questions that will elicit comments on the poise of your team.

CHAPTER 13

The Blueprint

The Master Plan

When Desmond found himself in the emergency room with pneumonia, he was surprised by the level of service he received. He was expecting a worst-case scenario: waiting for hours, getting little attention, and suffering among the gunshot victims. Instead, the staff was swift, respectful, and very caring. He and his family were treated with the utmost care from the moment he checked in, through various tests, and until he was discharged. He was pleasantly surprised and realized it was time to find a new doctor and practice that offered the same level of care as the emergency room.

The hospital put him in touch with a doctor who was part of the larger hospital practice, and Desmond was pleasantly surprised at the level of care he received there as well. The office was very clean and organized, and everyone he came in contact with was professional and kind. The doctor was on time for the appointment, was thoughtful, patient, and not rushed; the appointment lasted 45 minutes and every question Desmond had was addressed. His payment was accepted when he checked out, and he was offered a very warm good-bye and an offer to check in again if he had any questions.

I spoke to Jessica, the office manager of this busy medical practice to find out what its secret was; how did the employees ensure that the client received the best possible experience? She explained that "70 percent of our clients arrive to our office when they are quite ill; they don't feel well and are often a bit cranky. It is our job to turn them around and make them comfortable. We train the staff on welcoming the patient, getting him comfortable, and offering him a glass of water. We also train the team on interacting with the patients and knowing when to get a supervisor when they have a patient who is in immediate need." Jessica has set up a number of "service guidelines" (like the ones listed above) for her team to follow. Everyone receives training on these guidelines, and the hospital also offers many additional service classes for the staff. In this office, training is ongoing.

The practice's service credo is that "everyone is treated like a VIP," and every patient is given proper time and attention when he or she is in the office or calling on the phone. Jessica hires staff members who are customer-focused, who already believe that "the customer is always right," and she often hires people with retail backgrounds because this mind-set has been instilled in them. Moreover, the practice invests in a lot of staff training so that every patient receives the best care and has the most positive experience when at the office. Jessica also has dedicated desk staff and separate phone staff. This allows staff members to focus on the patient in front of them or on the line. The members of the desk staff will not be distracted from their patient because the phone rings, and this ensures that the patient gets the staff person's full attention.

Jessica shares this nugget of wisdom with her staff: "Don't let the last interaction influence the current interaction." That is, if your previous patient was challenging, you must shake this off and present yourself with a fresh perspective and positive energy to the person in front of you. "Everyone," she says, "is here for the patient. That's why we're all in health care, we want to see people thrive." This level of customer service was felt by Desmond in the last place he expected it: the doctor's office.

You must have guidelines for your service. Service is a system that will impact every moment with each of your guests. Your service system will address your service needs and articulate the experience you want to create for your customers. A well-thought-out system will also demonstrate how your staff members fit into the experience and how many staff members you will require to carry out each moment of the service interaction. Building your service plan, the service "blueprint," allows you to consider the guest experience, the staff experience, the design, and the layout through the little moments that demonstrate how service will work in action.

Restaurants regularly develop a blueprint for service called "The Steps of Service" or "The Sequence of Service." It lays out the service experience step by step, from the first moment the guest interacts with the business until the last. In full-service dining this blueprint begins with the moment the guest calls the restaurant to reserve a table and then maps out every moment the guest has while in the restaurant. Guest arrival, greeting at the host stand, seating, offering menus, greeting the guest at the table, pouring water, offering beverages, and serving bread are all separate "steps" that must be considered both on their own and as part of the larger experience. This consideration ensures that nothing gets left out and that the staff covers all bases. This blueprint helps define not only the guest's experience but also shows how all members of the service staff fit into this experience.

For example, I have my students write out the steps of service for a potential business in order to see how it impacts their labor cost. Often, people have grand ideas about service; they conjure up many specialized interactions that require many different types of staff members. And this adds up fast. On the other hand, managers often have ideas that their employees can handle many of the steps on their own. But how can one person take care of a client, answer the phone, receive the merchandise, and set up the showroom? In this case more people are needed so that the staff can properly handle all the aspects of the operation and all the intricacies of service. The steps of service, your essential service plan, are a great way to understand how to make service happen and how to involve your staff.

In businesses with a large phone-based customer service operation, you will create a "service script" for the operators to follow. In other businesses you might also create the "client journey" or "guest experience" as an outline of how you will treat your customers when they are interacting with your business and your teams. Every company should focus on each moment of service so that there are no surprises. Often, businesses with a receptionist or reception area assume that their staff in this area will be kind and nice and thoughtful. And most of the time that is true. But by offering an outline for those staff members to follow, you are ensuring two things for your clients: consistency and opportunity. Consistency is key to the service equation, and it is what most guests are seeking. Opportunity has two faces: one is the opportunity to connect and comprehend your guests a little better, and the second is that there is an opportunity to create more sales by offering options and upgrades.

When planning your new business you must consider the service and how it will be achieved under your roof. First you must identify the goal of service, what experience you hope to deliver, and who will be involved. Then you must decide how the service will be communicated and performed in the space. Finally, you will develop a space that is conducive to the service you wish to deliver and the experience you want your guests to remember.

Moment by Moment

In the steps of service it is important to outline who is carrying out each step and how it must be done. I like to give examples that are specific to the business and list the little details that will impact this "moment of service." This helps train the staff member who is responsible for the guest experience in this particular moment. I like to use each moment of service as a how-to for each moment that the staff and guest may interact. The moment could be conducted over the phone, in person, speaking, or not speaking. Each moment is singular and important, and this is why you must write out all moments for yourself and then for your staff.

When figuring out the steps of service, you have to start with your goal. It could be to make a sale, to share products, or to solve problems. When outlining how to make a sale you may consider the following steps:

- greeting
- introduction of goods/services
- description of options
- upselling
- taking the order
- delivery of the product

- payment
- thank you
- farewell

And if you are meeting a new client and are telling that person about options or services, you may change your steps to reflect the following scenario:

- greeting
- assessment of needs
- framing of needs and recommendation of products
- description of options
- description of next steps
- thank you
- farewell

If you are solving clients' problems, you will be tweaking that list as follows:

- greeting
- assessment of needs
- framing of needs and recommendation of solutions
- adapting solution
- getting help if needed
- description of next steps
- thank you
- farewell

These outlines are similar in that each has the essential ingredients: greeting, thank you, farewell, and in the middle each has a conversation about the client's needs and solutions for that need. There are a number of considerations when building your steps of service:

- name of the service moment
- the goal of the moment
- time (when it should happen or the duration of the moment)

- who is involved
- verbiage style
- what is essential to the business at this step
- what is essential to the customer at this step
- what are common interferences with this step
- how to handle common problems
- when to involve others
- upselling or marketing opportunities
- how to complete this moment

Let's build a step of service together using the example of the greeting, our first and most important step of service. You can name this moment "The greeting," or you could call it "addressing the guest" or "answering the phone." You must decide on the goal of the greeting, and it will likely be to address the guest in a friendly and professional manner, welcoming the guest into your business. The greeting should have a time consideration, not for duration of the moment itself (other steps may have a duration), but rather for the time it should take for a guest to get greeted. For one client I wrote this as part of the "greeting" moment of service:

The 3-Second Rule: if you greet someone within 3 seconds of seeing him/her you are more likely to do so authentically and with energy. If you wait, then you will think about it too much. Be swift and say hello!

In each step it is essential to let people know who is involved. In the case of the greeting, I usually include "all staff," but there might be points on the journey (first greeting, second greeting) where one person will be responsible for that particular moment of greeting the guests. You may specify that the "receptionist" conducts the first greeting and that the "assistant" greets the client upon arrival at the specific office.

The way you offer the greeting is of the utmost importance, and your choice of verbiage is key in unifying the staff and enunciating your brand consistently. This is also an opportunity to speak about the vision of the business as well as the expectation of the client. This is what I added to another greeting for a client to address the business goal while also speaking about the guest experience:

It is difficult speaking to strangers, but in the spirit of being a good neighbor we must be gracious and welcoming to everyone who enters our store. We must acknowledge everyone because they are our customers, and they provide our livelihood by making purchases here rather than somewhere else. We show that we value our customers by the kindness and friendliness that we demonstrate.

If there are any moments where a problem might occur, then you must give staff members options for handling such an occurrence. While you don't want to convey the idea that every moment will be fraught with issues, you must offer ways to approach strangers even when there might be a difficulty. For example, you might ask clients if there is anything else you should know about their call or visit or if they have visited you before so you can understand their needs a little better.

Here is an example of the "greeting" I wrote for a hotel restaurant client. It contains all the little sections above and gives examples of how to conduct the moment and interact with the guest and with colleagues:

- **Hospitality coordinator greets the guest:**
  - Welcomes party to the restaurant: "Good Morning! Welcome!"
  - Receives the party: "What is the name of your reservation this morning?" or "did you reserve with us this morning?"
    - Note: use care when asking guests if they have booked a table; we don't want to give the impression that we require reservations but that we are able to seat guests even without a booking.
  - If the party has no reservation, be sure to take the reservation name "May I have your name for our reservation book? Thank you!"

- If you know the guest's name, then please use it each time you address the guest. Do your best to memorize guest's names and address them by name for an amazing moment of guest recognition.
  - The hospitality coordinator makes notes in the reservation system: partially arrived, all arrived.
  - Prior to seating the guest, the hospitality coordinator prints out a Guest Information Ticket to give to the server and manager when the party is seated for enhanced guest recognition.
  - If partially arrived, inquire if the guest would prefer to wait at the table (if available) or in the lobby for the rest of the party "would you like to go ahead to the table or wait for your guests in the lobby?"
  - If fully arrived, ask if they are ready to be seated: "your table is all ready; may I take you there? Please follow me this way."
  - If guest has coats, umbrellas, packages, or bags, then the hospitality coordinator directs guests to a coat check coordinator: "If you would like to check your things, Donna will take them for you."

In sales moments you want to give your staff examples of appropriate "upselling" or "suggestive selling," that is, you should train them in how to offer another product as a companion to the product at hand. Upselling is a great thing for the bottom line, but you must give examples of how to do so in a way that is perceived as helpful (serving a need) rather than pushy (forcing a product on customers in order to make more money.) For example, for a bakery client I wrote the following script about upselling:

Before they [customers] pay, remember to upsell the products in your department. Upselling is a way to introduce customers to products that they might enjoy while also adding to the total sale in your department. It is always important to use a helpful and informative tone so the customer doesn't feel "pushed" to buy another item.

For example:

"If you like, the ginger scone is amazing with tea. Absolutely delicious!"

"If you get a chance, you should try one of our new scones, they go great with afternoon tea!"

"We just added a new type of scone, ginger-oatmeal. Let me know if you would like to try one today."

You must be clear on what language is acceptable and properly represents the brand by writing out examples of your brand language. As we discussed in chapter 5, how you say something carries meaning that makes an impression on your guests. Giving examples of how to handle various situations in the steps of service is very helpful for the staff; by giving examples you are letting your teams know what is expected of them. For instance, it is helpful to outline how common situations should be handled. For someone confirming appointments or reservations there are two possible scenarios: you leave a message or speak to a real person. Each scenario has a different script. For example:

Voicemail message: "Good morning/afternoon, this is [your name] from [XYZ business] calling regarding your appointment tomorrow at 1 p.m. Please call us back at 866–555–1212 to let us know if you must cancel or change your appointment. Otherwise we look forward to seeing you then. Thank you and have a good day."

- Live person: "Good afternoon/evening, this is [your name] from [XYZ business]. May I speak with Mr. Jones?"
  - Mr. Jones: "This is he."
- "Great! I'm calling to confirm your appointment at 1 p.m. tomorrow with [name of person]. May I confirm that for you?"
  - Mr. Jones: "Yes, I will be there."
  - If not Mr. Jones: "Please let Mr. Jones know I will be calling back later to confirm his appointment. Thanks and have a great day!"
- "Thank you, we look forward to seeing you then. Good bye!"
  - Or if canceling: "Thank you for letting us know, may I reschedule your appointment for you?"

You have to arm your teams with examples, possibilities, and training regarding how to interact with your guests. Even the farewell or good-bye is something that must be practiced and perfected. The good-bye is an important moment as it serves to tie up the experience "with a bow" (aka in a nice way.) That moment creates a lasting final impression of your brand so how you tie the bow verbally is of the utmost importance. I always say that staff members can't say good-bye or thank-you too often and train the entire team to take a moment to thank every passing guest as he or she is leaving. This ensures a positive last impression of the brand and the customer's service experience.

Telecommunications

Customer service that is conducted over the phone can be very limited. All you have are your words and the ticking clock: the time it takes to speak to a representative and make a purchase, get questions answered, or have problems solved. Every second matters, and every word has a resonance that is enhanced in this setting. When a national weight loss chain decided to add an interactive method of coaching clients in the process of weight loss, the company strove to formulate a way to reach its customers that was authentic, helpful, and would truly invite people to call in. Weight loss is fraught with challenges. This company realized that if it could offer support over the phone, then maybe its clients would be more successful.

The company built a 24/7 phone service its clients could call to access weight loss coaches who were on hand to help and support members as they worked toward their goal. Company executives identified three areas of interaction for the clients: when clients have cheated on their diet, when clients are faced with cheating and need help to stay on track, and when clients have had a successful day or moment to share and record. Once these moments were established, the company retained a "service script doctor" to outline the moments of service on the phone when clients call in.

The challenge of the phone calls was to ensure that the clients felt supported through all these possible moments while the goal of weight loss was preserved. The company developed brand standards for the phone calls and partnered with the script doctor to develop service scripts for the phone operators. The scripts included a number of traits for the operators to embody: empathetic, credible, friendly, practical, relatable, and nonjudgmental. The scripts also included various moments of service: starting the call, engaging the client, providing helpful tips, and ending the call. Throughout the script were examples of how to engage with the client at each moment of the conversation, and in each script there were options for how to handle problems, issues, and common client difficulties.

The goal for all calls was to help clients successfully complete the program. The operator was prompted in the script to refer to past successful moments to remind the client of having done well in the past while also referring to the client's ultimate goal: reaching the desired weight loss number. The process of losing weight is very personal, and for some it is quite shameful; for this company it was key that the operators were also on the plan. This offered assurance that the person answering the call could truly relate to the customers and offer help and winning tips for success. The language was also detailed in the script with words and examples that exemplified the above traits. "Wow, Emma, sounds like you have been through a lot." Or "Well, based on what you shared with me, I think we have some options that could really be useful and help you shed some pounds." All examples were designed to fit the goal of the call while upholding the brand attributes and specific needs of the client on the line.

A Space Odyssey

Space is a key consideration in building a new business because your budget will limit the total space you can afford. But be warned: too much space is as much as a hindrance as too little. When you have a spacious area for the guest experience, you must consider how your staff will utilize the space as well. Are the storage areas accessible without staff having to disappear for minutes at a time? How long does it take for a staff member to greet a guest or answer the phone? More space literally equals more steps for your staff to take. By creating a blueprint of service, you can anticipate the needs of your business and the requirements of the service experience you want to occur in that space. If your operation is in smaller confines, then efficiency is of a great concern. Making it possible for your teams to take fewer steps to accomplish their job while they interact with their clients is the goal when space is at a minimum.

For example, I had a client who took a space that was 350 square feet, and the design was finely tuned in order to maximize output of the teams while creating a unique and efficient service experience for the guests.

Storage is a big concern when developing a space that that is conducive to serving your guests. How your teams access documents, products, and packaging is a key concern as it affects the number of steps they must take when helping their guests and thus impacts their efficiency. Having an efficient experience (the timing of the experience) is something that is a priority for most consumers. And being able to serve your guests properly will help your staff stay positive and offer a great experience for your guest.

Organization and presentation of your merchandise will also affect the service experience. Being able to find what is desired will keep customers satisfied and an organized flow of products promotes a positive impression of the business and improves sales. Ease in your space is a key consideration for your guests as this impacts the customer experience (as discussed in chapter 3); therefore, you must "walk through" the experience on paper first. Writing out the customer journey on paper can make a huge difference in the experience that your guest has while in your space.

For example, flow is a major concern and is one of the focuses of the blueprint of service. Flow refers to how people move through your space and how they experience your business, brand, and products. When designing its interactive stores, Apple looked at the flow of their stores and created a system that maximized flow and customer/staff interaction. Apple stores are designed with three distinct areas: the Red Zone, which is where all the products are displayed, the Family Zone where people can get a demonstration on how to utilize a new Apple product and where products for kids are displayed, and the Genius Bar where people go to get help with their current products. Each area is designed to maximize flow while offering products for sale. The Red Zone is created with an open floor plan to encourage movement and browsing. The Family Zone has seats for guests and their families as well as products that are displayed at kids' eye level to encourage spending on children's products. The Genius Bar was designed based on a concierge desk at the Ritz Carlton; it offers seating for those waiting and for those who are engaging with a "genius" or tech consultant, and there is digital signage that displays the status on your time in line and indicates who is next in the queue.

The Apple store also has roaming salespeople who interact with guests in all the areas. They can answer product questions as well as offer ideas for adding additional products to customers' purchases. Each salesperson has a handheld computer for checking on stock and availability. This makes "making a sale" immediate and helps each associate make suggestions for customers. The handheld devices also accept credit card payments and "runners" bring products from the storeroom to the sales floor, expediting the checkout process. Apple outlined the service the company wanted to deliver to guests, and this helped executives articulate the sales model that utilizes a roaming salesperson and a product runner. Without this consideration there would have been no innovation in the checkout process; this innovation—a handheld POS device—has revolutionized retail sales by going to customers in the moment of making a choice rather than having them leave the sales floor to check out. Innovations in service start with your goal: to serve as many people as efficiently and memorably as possible.

In many businesses, however, service and design are an afterthought. If service isn't a consideration when you are building your operation, then it may not work as well as you intend it to once the space has been completed. In my experience a new business will show me the completed and approved blueprint and design plans and then ask what I think of the design. Too often, unfortunately, the design is an impediment to the service the business wants to offer. Service is most often impaired because the form and design of the space have eclipsed the function of the business. I have consulted with many clients and businesses that have a challenging space to work with and every time I wish I had been called in sooner to point out little fixes that would have a big impact on the service experience.

Service is a system that needs clear articulation, as it will be impacted by the entire layout of the business. For example, you must first identify the guest experience and then make sure the designer can capture that in the space you are configuring. This is where the "blueprint of service" comes in so handy; this outline will demonstrate the goal of the space and help make service possible throughout your business.

Tips and Takeaways

- **See and Share the Future.** As a manager or leader your main job is to share and uphold your company's vision and set goals regarding it. If the vision is to deliver a great service program, then it is your job to address it as you build your concept and write your business plan. It is never too early to develop your vision around service because it is the thing you will eventually spend much time on. When your vision has been clearly articulated through your service blueprint, then it will be easier for your team members to help deliver it to your guests. They will be trained and empowered to bring your vision to life.

- **Tune In.** Take time to observe and listen to your team members to ensure that they are upholding the service standards you have created. Pay attention to staff members who are especially good at their job or have a particular skill in handling specific challenges or service moments. These are the people who can help you make changes to the scripts you are already using, and their facility with client engagement can help you make your service systems better than ever.

- **Stay Current.** Once you have written the service blueprint for your business, it is essential to update it when changes are made. Make sure it is complete and up-to-date each time a new hire is brought on board so that your vision of service can be properly expressed and explained to each new staff member.

- **Diversify.** Training your team is always important but it is especially important for trainees to be able to observe and listen to as many other seasoned staff as possible before conversing with the public. Your team will have various ways of handling situations and engaging guests, and the best staff members will have a comfort and ease that your new team members can aspire to. More than one person should always conduct training in order to demonstrate different styles of delivering the company message. Give your new team members the opportunity to work with and observe the best brand ambassadors you have on staff.

CHAPTER 14

Every Time I Say Good-Bye

Touchpoints

Frank Bruni, the former restaurant reviewer of the *NY Times,* once wrote a review of the restaurant Benoit, located in New York City. The restaurant pays homage to France and French tradition and is owned by one of the most venerated French chefs, Alain Ducasse. The review was memorable, not because of what he said about the food and beautiful interior, but because of what he said about his final moment of service: the good-bye. In the article entitled "A Museum of Familiar French," published on July 9, 2008, Bruni began his review with a description of this moment:

> One of my most memorable experiences—a telling one, too—came not while I was on a red velvet banquette in the dining room...but while I was on my way out the door. A hostess called after my companions and me. She wanted to bid us adieu. Except it wasn't adieu she bid.
>
> It was this: "Ciao!"
>
> Followed by this: "Grazie!"

He continued by describing the transformative experience of eating many classic French dishes in a traditional French manner. So the good-bye in Italian was a big misstep and led him to start off his review of the restaurant with this telling story: they're quite French but in the end, the good-bye and the experience came across as "false." Not an enviable sentiment despite the overall positive review.

Saying hello and good-bye are the bookends of a great experience. Hello sets the stage by being interactive and welcoming while good-bye serves to acknowledge the positive experience, is appreciative, and ties the service up with a bow. Hello creates a great first impression while good-bye acts as an echo of the good experience, creating a lasting final impression of your business. Leaving out the good-bye is a breach of customer service: it leaves the experience unfinished and the customer unacknowledged.

Like hello, good-bye is not a singular moment. There may be a few moments of good-bye as your guest leaves your establishment. Good-bye isn't just a word, either. It is a moment of service that includes a few important precursors that I call the four touchpoints. The moment of good-bye should include:

- recapping the experience and gaining feedback
- offering additional products or experiences to the customer
- genuine thanks
- heartfelt farewell

The good-bye moment is important as it allows you to truly and finally connect with your guest. In the restaurant business the typical good-bye sounds like this: "We're so glad you decided to celebrate with us tonight, how did your mother like her dessert? (Customer response) Is there anything else I might bring you? (Customer response.) Thank you so much, it was a pleasure seeing you all. Have a great night!" In this example each of the four touchpoints were addressed conversationally, and the entire good-bye flowed in natural progression. This happens all the time in other businesses as well and leaves customers feeling the experience was complete and ended appropriately.

When one of the touchpoints is missing, the good-bye can feel disjointed or strange. Many managers and employees do well with the second, third, and fourth touchpoint but ignore or leave out the first point: recapping and gaining feedback. One of the keys of successful customer service is that the customer leaves happy, and thus the staff members must ensure that happiness has been achieved. The only way to know this is by asking guests about their experience. Recently, I've noticed a number of retail stores commonly asking at the register, "Did you find everything you were looking for?" This question allows for feedback from the customer and is a moment that can increase the sale if an employee can find the item the customer was seeking and add it to the final sale.

Gaining feedback is important especially when your customers are still in your business. While they are still with you, you can offer an open ear, address any issues, solve problems, and make suggestions. You can also identify the customers who are happy in the moment and create a relationship with them based on their positive experience. This is also the moment to identify the guests who are not so happy and who feel their experience has fallen short. This is the moment to reel them back in with your service, attention, and products. You must capitalize on the moment your guests are still in the business because once they leave, they are much harder to reach. And when they leave disappointed, the memory they leave with is not so good, and this memory is hard to change.

Gaining feedback is helpful in making improvements to your business and makes the difference between guests having an average experience and having a positive one. Your guests experience your brand like no one else, so their point of view is incredibly valid. By checking in before they depart and asking for feedback, you may gain valuable insight, insight that can improve the experience of other guests as well. This is why this first touchpoint is an essential part of good-bye; it allows you to check in with your guests and ensure that they are satisfied with your brand.

The second touchpoint is also important as it piggybacks on the first. This is the moment when you can truly seal the deal by finding additional products or by making suggestions for the customers so that they may leave satisfied. This moment of engagement allows you to understand your guests' needs and discover where your business might be failing your guest while they are in the store. For instance if you ask "did you find everything ok?" your customer might say yes or they might tell you they came in for an item but it was not on the shelf. Once you start engaging your guests at this moment, you will start to see trends; you will discover the products that are most requested but not offered, and you will learn which are the items that are most frequently sold out. Seize this moment of good-bye to gain feedback about your offerings, your guests' experience, and their preferences. And take time to help your guests find and receive what they came in for in the first place.

The good-bye is an opportunity to exceed expectations by offering promotions or sales before the customers pay the bill. One company that does this well is the Gap. At the checkout the cashiers regularly inform customers about a sale or a promotion that is going on. For example, when I was buying socks there, the cashier told me that there was a promotion offering three pairs for $12, and if I wanted to I could get two more pairs of socks before paying. There was no worry that I would have to wait in line again; I was able to step away, choose two more items, and bring them to the cashier. The sale was increased but more than that my satisfaction was increased. By offering the promotion right before I was paying, the cashier made me feel considered; the store wanted me to get the best deal available. When I returned to the cashier, she was ready for me and was upbeat and glad I was able to take advantage of the promotion. This precursor to good-bye stayed in my mind, and my positive experience turned into positive memories of the Gap.

The Gratitude Factor

The third touch point is thank you. This moment is so important as you must thank your guests for purchasing and for visiting. I always say there is no such thing as saying thank you too often and a chorus of "thank you" and "good-bye" is a wonderful ending to the customers' experience. The thank-you must be sincere, and your employees must engage with the customer, maintain eye contact, and be direct in their salutation. "Thank you for coming," "Thanks so much for joining us today," or "Thank you so much" are all options that get the point across nicely. Your team must show gratitude to your guests; they are the reason you are in business.

God's Love We Deliver (GLWD) is a nonprofit organization with the mission to bring fresh meals to people who are homebound with life-threatening illness. With thousands of clients to feed, the organization relies heavily on donors and volunteers. Stephen Covello is the manager of corporate partnerships and key donors, and for him gratitude is where it's at. Recently, he helped launch the Gratitude Project with the goal to reach out to the organization's donors and volunteers to thank them. The project had a bit of a rocky start, however, as the program was launched by telephone. "In the nonprofit world, phone calls have a bad reputation...most people assume that we are calling to ask for money so we had to create a script that got our volunteers right to the point."

The script Stephen wrote is made up of three points: introduction, thank you, and good-bye. The introduction is a succinct "Hello, I'm a volunteer with God's Love We Deliver." Then the volunteer moves quickly on to the message of thanks ("We just called to say thank you so much for all you do") and Stephen says that "the person receiving the call is often surprised that this is all we called to say." Then the call wraps up with a continuation of the relationship. "I always want to continue our connection by saying 'until next time' or 'hope to see you soon' or even just 'have a great weekend," Steven shared. I never say 'good-bye' as it feels too final." And the success of GLWD is that its donors are also its volunteers; the relationship is sure to continue on many levels in the years ahead.

The Gratitude Project has made over 4,000 calls just to say "thank you." And the nonprofit also takes time to thank their volunteers by sending out grateful birthday cards. "We each write something on the birthday cards, and we send out about 8,000 a year. That's a lot of birthdays but 95 percent of the total work is accomplished by our volunteers." Stephen says the cards are important because "in man hours that is equal to $2 million dollars saved in payroll." Clearly, gratitude is at the heart of this business, and taking time to connect to donors and volunteers keeps the message alive and the mission active for the many clients that rely on them daily.

"Thank you" is one of the most positive things you can say to your customers. It completes the sales moment with appreciation for the transaction and places the focus on your customers, their actions, and their value to you and your business. Saying thank you is a two-way street: it positively acknowledges the customer while becoming a positive moment for your staff member as well. As it turns out, gratitude is powerful and developing a culture of gratitude can improve your life—and your business—in magical ways.

Robert A. Emmons is a gratitude expert who has written two books on the topic. In researching gratitude he has discovered that fostering gratitude can impact your health; it can improve your psychological well-being and social abilities. In his article posted on the Greater Good website entitled "Why Gratitude is Good," Emmons explains that "gratitude is a social emotion because it requires us to see how we've been supported and affirmed by other people."[1] Gratitude is not solitary; it is giving thanks and acknowledgement to someone for having an impact on your life. In business, gratitude means thanking and acknowledging your customers for having an impact on your business. One doesn't happen without the other; the sale would not have happened without the support of your customer.

"Gratitude allows us to celebrate the present," says Emmons. He explains that research shows that positive emotions wear off quickly. The high of making a sale is a fleeting feeling of positivity. "But gratitude makes us appreciate the value of something, and when we appreciate the value of something, we extract more benefits from it" and, Eammons continues, "we're less likely to take it for granted." When businesses truly value their customers and demonstrate their gratitude, they are able to prolong the good feelings their customers feel by adding value and thus enhancing the positive experience of making the sale.

Gratitude also matters in regard to your teams. By building a culture of valuing gratitude and thanking your customers and employees, you will let your teams feel the impact of being grateful at work. Because gratitude is a social emotion, it helps focus us on the positive, which, in turn, helps block negative emotions. As Dr. Emmons explains, "You cannot feel envious and grateful at the same time. They're incompatible feelings." Therefore, by encouraging a grateful workplace where employees focus on the positive, demonstrating gratitude to their customers for supporting your business and making their livelihood possible, you are helping your teams to boost their own positive emotions while at work. And having grateful and positive emotions helps us block stress and keep negativity at bay.

Emmons also acknowledges that cultivating gratitude is not easy and recommends keeping a gratitude journal and taking time in the morning or evening to connect with the things and people you are grateful for in your day. I think that by encouraging gratitude at work you can help your teams see how important they are to one another and come to truly value your customers for making all of our jobs possible. As an example, consider this story Emmons shares in his article:

> Mother Theresa talked about how grateful she was to the people she was helping, the sick and dying in the slums of Calcutta, because they enabled her to grow and deepen her spirituality. That's a very different way of thinking about gratitude—gratitude for what we can give as opposed to what we receive.[2]

This is the real stuff. Those of us who work in customer service know our job is to impact strangers and create a personalized experience for other people. And in doing so we are able to create satisfaction in doing a great job, listening well, and making others happy. Service is somewhat selfless as our job is to make the lives of others better. But there is deep happiness to be gained, and the above story illustrates this. Our strength and success in business is about serving others. This is where the true impact of service lies, and when we can be grateful for this relationship, the satisfaction and happiness know no end.

Saying thank you is a representation of our gratitude. There are two inherent parts to thank -you: the gratitude part and the "you" part. The "you" part has an impact as well because "you" is one of the most persuasive words in the English language. It tops the list every year and is so persuasive because you are focusing on the other person, making that person the star. But "you" has still more power than that. Anyone can make the "you" even more personal by replacing it with a name, and this has been proven to have profound results. In a study conducted by Dennis P. Carmody and Michael Lewis called "Brain Activation When Hearing One's Own and Others' Names," participants monitored by an MRI demonstrated increased brain activity when their name was spoken versus when it was omitted. As it turns out, using someone's name gets the person's attention as nothing else does.

Thus, consider the moment of thanking your guest. You can certainly say "thank you," and it will be a positive experience. But saying "thank you so much, Renee" or "we really appreciate your business Ms. Lynch" will resonate with your guest more than anything. Again, it is about creating memories and lasting impressions, and this is where thank you and good-bye are so valuable in ending the customers' experience.

Until We Meet Again

The fourth touchpoint is the actual good-bye. Depending on your company culture, you could say good-bye in another language (see above for being in alignment with your brand) or use a shortened "bye" as your guests depart. Often thank-you and good-bye are used interchangeably with some employees saying "good-bye" while others say "thank you." While this is okay, you must still have one moment of thank-you as well as a moment of good-bye. Gratitude connects our actions with your staff and guests. Good-bye seals the deal on making a lasting impression. It is the last thing you give to your clients, and it will stay in their memory as they leave.

Good-bye can be physical as well as verbal. Holding the door open while saying good-bye is a very gracious gesture that can make a big impression. At a restaurant I frequent, the host staff always says good-bye as they open and hold the door for me as I depart, and this makes me feel considered. This is an "I notice = I care" moment brought to life that is attached to the very last moment I am in this business. Another physical demonstration of good-bye is to step around the sales desk to say good-bye to the customer. This can be done in order to personally hand the guest the merchandise, or it can be done to interact more closely by offering a handshake together with a verbal farewell. Both physical interactions are active and intentional, two aspects of great customer service.

Good-bye is something you must consider on a deeper level as well. Many people do not like good-byes because they signify a parting and, potentially, an ending. In his book *Transitions: Making Sense of Life's Changes,* William Bridges speaks about the intensity of the endings people all share. "Considering that we have to deal with endings all of our lives, most of us handle them poorly," he says; we "take them either too seriously or not seriously enough." He believes most people take endings "too seriously by confusing them with finality—that's it, all over, never more, finished!"[3] In customer service this is a confusion that must be confronted and then avoided at all costs. Good-bye is not an ending but the completion of one moment that can lead to another. It is the bait that can keep your customer interested and ensure that your business is established firmly in the guest's memory as a place that is available when needed.

You must remind yourself that good-bye is not final. You must keep a virtual tether to each of your guests by keeping your business in their minds and memories. After your guests have left your business, there are so many ways to stay connected to them. Many businesses send out newsletters and updates as a way to stay connected and bring their customers back. Many offer promotions or sales to give people a great reason to return. Some create a community for their clients to engage in long after they have left the premises.

For example, Finish Line Physical Therapy is a practice that is dedicated to athletes of all kinds, and the company's service is focused on helping patients achieve their goals and recover as swiftly as possible. Andre Fries, the office manager, works hard to keep connected to the practice's many clients, and he and the owner, Michael Conlon, have built a community based on a shared love of sports. "Everyone working at Finish Line is an athlete as well," says Andre; "we see our patients on the race course, and we share the same enthusiasm for sports as our patients."

The practice sends out regular newsletters and hosts weekly events that are free to attend. Staff members or guests host the events and cover topics from an introduction to bike racing and the benefits of foam rolling and they even offer a barefoot workout. This community of health and wellness represents one of the underlying goals. "The bottom line," Andre shares, "is that we all care and want to see our patients achieve their goals." Hosting ongoing and regular events keeps the focus on health, strength, and wellness, which is a strong connection for the company's patients.

Finish Line likes to keep patients involved in the business even when they are physically fully recovered. The owners sponsor races and even have a yearly cornhole contest to create some fun on a Saturday afternoon and raise funds for a needy charity. Staff members are encouraged to connect with their patients after their recovery; some connect on Linked in or Facebook to keep the relationship current. Some share race and competition information with their clients who are looking for a new event or course to try out. Some clients use the company's services pro-actively as they approach a big race or competition and see Finish Line as a partner in their athletic pursuits. Finish Line's blog features articles about how to begin a new sport and also addresses common physical ail-ments. This diversity of health and prevention information ensures that patients remain engaged with the physical therapy practice whether they are injured or not.

When patients are checking out after a session, the reception team always engages them on the status of their latest race or asks about upcoming events that the patients are participating in. This moment is about relating one-on-one with a fellow athlete while making an appointment for follow-up care. At the same time the Finish Line staff acknowledges the moment at hand with congratulations for achieving recovery or understanding as patients progress through the pain.

"We have relationships with our clients that are long lasting. Some cli-ents are working through an injury or are preparing for a competition, so they may have weekly or twice-weekly appointments. Some may need a monthly maintenance appointment, and others may want an occasional tune-up." Andre refers to his team and patients as the Finish Line family and this includes the staff, patients, the patients' coaches and doctors, and also includes Miles, the practice's golden retriever and mascot. Keeping patients connected to the Finish Line community helps ensure that the relationship is ongoing and continued, both when patients are injured and when they are in good health.

Auf Wiedersehen

Heidi Klum is a supermodel and a media titan. She has built an empire around a number of TV shows that are filmed internationally. The shows (*Project Runway* is the American version) are a competition where fashion designers compete weekly for the ultimate award of winning $100,000 to start their own fashion label. Ms. Klum oversees the weekly competition with one loser getting cut at the end of each weekly episode. In her most imperious Teutonic voice she bids the poor contestant *"auf Wiedersehen,"* a phrase that represents the finality of the moment. But what is funny about this is that *"auf Wiedersehen"* actually means "see you again" and so is anything but final. The situation, being sent home by a German super-star, is what gives this stern good-bye its muscle rather than the words themselves.

There are many options when saying good-bye. Many regional or inter-national businesses use their native language when bidding farewell to their customers. In many languages "good-bye" is actually a positive salutation, a wish for safety or luck in the day of those departing. *"Auf Wiedersehen"* and *"au revoir"* are both roughly equal to "until we see each other again." No finality is implied at all. Our very own "good-bye" is the shortened ver-sion of a phrase that was popular in the sixteenth century meaning "God be with you." It is an exclamation that signifies a parting, a leaving, or a farewell with the hope that the one leaving is looked after and kept safe. "Good-bye" was originally meant as a salutation and a good wish. We com-monly wish people well when they leave us with salutations like "take care," "be well," "have a good day," and "good night/afternoon/morning/day." All are wishing the recipient well, and all are positive and friendly ways to sign off.

In business, too, you must be proactive about your good-bye; it is not an ending but a warm completion of a service moment that your customers would love to repeat again and often. Adding a warm salutation is helpful in a moment that otherwise could be fraught with emotion. "We'll see you again soon," "enjoy your [name of product]," or "please visit us again"—all these help warm up this final moment and connect the customers to our business once more. The good-bye is your opportunity to ensure that satis-faction has been achieved, that all products have been offered, that gratitude is expressed, and that you are connecting with your guests in a way that creates a permanent bond between customer and company. Your action and intention toward your customers in that moment is loud and clear: your experience matters to us, and we are grateful for your business.

Tips and Takeaways

- **Support Your Team**. Support and help your teams when they are conducting "good-bye." You can help team members by being present, asking for feedback, retrieving more products, and creating that lasting memory as customers depart through your door. Let your staff members lead the way and support them as they conduct each of these moments of service with your guests; let your team members be the superstars your guests will remember.

- **Solidify the Last Impression**. Don't run away from good-bye! Create the tether that will bring your guests back another time. And train your staff members so that everyone is able to engage the guests as they are leaving. Helping guests with their packages, packing their shopping bags, holding the door open for them—these are all nonverbal ways to connect and create the positive last memory of your business.

- **Make a Connection**. Most managers are given branded business cards with their name, position and contact information. Ask them to give it out to their customers as a way to create a tie with your business. Encourage your managers to personalize a moment of good-bye by offering their card as a way to stay in touch, get information or solve issues for their customers. Train them to ask for their client's cards as well so that they can follow up with an email to say hello, follow up on their experience and make your business a little more approachable.

- **Community Impact**. Consider how you can create and encourage a community based on your business. Many businesses think of this as being a marketing initiative, and it is, but it also serves to keep the service conversation going. Hosting events or supporting a charity is a great way to be involved in a good cause while inviting your community into the event as a participant or as an attendee. I know financial planners and lawyers who regularly host informational events about various topics that are informative for their clients and keep the latter connected to the firm. Remember that good-bye is not final but is a moment for us to say "see you soon." By creating additional ways to see customers we are acting on that promise.

CHAPTER 15

The Manager of Small Things

Creating an Experience

The social kiss, once or twice on the cheek, is a lovely greeting that is quite continental. At Balthazar, a classic French restaurant, the French staff naturally greeted one another with two kisses when starting or finishing work. The rest of the staff adopted this cultural ritual and greeted one another this way, and the managers also greeted regular guests with familiar, social kisses. The challenge was in knowing how many kisses for each guest. For born and bred New Yorkers it is one kiss on the cheek with as little lip as possible. Call it a "jawbone" kiss with a quick press of the lower cheeks. Then for the continental types from Europe it is two kisses, one on each cheek, right side first then left. Now if your guest is Swiss there may be three kisses: right, left, right. Or on occasion you may find a Swiss four-kisser: right, left, right, left. The challenge is anticipating what is natural for the guest in front of you and keeping your poise if and when you go for the unannounced second side when the guest is expecting only one and is caught unawares.

The social kissing I describe is not just about an international greeting; it is about creating an experience for our guests that felt like a true French escapade. As managers we started out the guests' experience by welcoming guests in a way that was different from what other restaurants were doing. This kiss was a message to our guests that let them know they had entered another environment, one where the welcome is warm, the food is delicious, and the experience is transporting. Our job as managers was to create an authentic experience by living it and sharing it with our guests and staff.

At Balthazar I was a manager, and my title was maître d'. "Maître d'" is short for "maître d'hotel" and translates literally to "master of the house." In the restaurant business, this person is generally recognized as the one in charge or the one who runs the service. I held this role for many years at many restaurants in the course of my career, and as maître d' I was the "face" of each business as I was there to welcome and greet every guest of each restaurant, with warmth, with kindness, and, sometimes, with a kiss.

But being maître d' is not about kissing people. It is about standing up for the restaurant, representing its identity with every word and every decision. A good maître d' drives the guest experience while keeping an eye on the purse strings of the restaurant, and she demonstrates this with every guest she seats. This position is entrusted with making money for the business by seating enough people so that they all receive the experience they seek and thus generate income for the business. I loved this front row seat to service and contributing to the business of a successful restaurant. I learned many lessons, for example, how to speak to people to set their expectations and how to solve problems for guests and staff. This position was my proving ground and allowed me to earn my virtual master's degree in the intricacies of service.

Every manager should consider himself or herself the "master of the house," and owners should empower their managers to take charge, be responsible, and make informed decisions for the business. As maître d' I made hundreds of decisions a night that impacted the guests' experience and involved the staff. There are literally thousands of little things that we, the managers, must see, do, consider, weigh, make actionable, and follow up on. There are many ways managers can impact service and guide the staff. As managers, we set the direction and tone of the day, and if we don't focus on the little things that matter, who will? We must understand that our job is to create, uphold, and maintain an experience that will make the customers happy and bring them back. It is all within our power, and it is very satisfying when we do it well.

Hello to You!

Through each chapter we have looked at how little things impact the service experience of the guest. And each of these little things is something we can also use with the staff. Let's start with hello, the first important facet of service. This is an important piece of the service experience, but it is also a key part of being a manager and being in charge. When you say hello to your staff members, you get their attention, tell them you are there, set the tone for the day, and interact with the employees in a small but meaningful way. Saying hello and greeting your team tells them that you are energized and are on duty, ready for the shift ahead.

When I was a manager, I would walk through the various areas of the operation and check in with everyone by saying "hello," "good morning," or "good afternoon." I would take a moment to check in and get status on the day ahead or check on the finish of the service before. This gave me information but also kept the staff members on their toes: they had to be ready with the information that I would invariably ask for. I would walk through and check various areas of the operation to check for organization, cleanliness, and preparation; when something was out of place or amiss, I would greet the next staff member I saw and tell that person my observation in order to get him or her to fix the issue at hand.

My modus operandi when greeting the staff was to demonstrate my energy for my job. I was upbeat, smiling, warm, and often greeted my colleagues with a handshake. If I was energized and smiling, it was infectious. As I shared in chapter 12, my poise and energy would literally be transferred to others, setting the tone for the day. I worked with a manager back in the nineties who really made an impression on me. He always arrived at work with a smile and a bounce in his step. He was gracious and warm and always dressed impeccably; his tie was tied perfectly and his shoes were always polished. He always had a kind word for us as he made his rounds and had a twinkle in his eyes. This served to inspire us: we stood up straight in his presence, smiled authentically, and demonstrated that we knew our job. It was a wonderful feeling when he arrived on the job, and his spirit truly uplifted us at the start of our day.

As you make your rounds, you must keep your eyes open. What is in need of attention or repair? What needs to be organized or improved? What are you seeing that needs to be shared so that the team can see it too? As a manager, you must get results from your team. You will lead by example, but you must also lead a horse to water by sharing your expectations and goals with your team. Leading by example is crucial as it helps to express the expectation. You must be clear and precise in sharing and communicating your expectation to begin with. I always work with my clients on how to get results from their staff. First: share the vision or the goal. Second: tell staff members how they are involved in the goal. Third: give a timeline for achieving the goal. Finally: acknowledge when they have achieved the goal.

For instance, I had a client who was bothered that the displays of fruit near the entrance were always half full. He told his manager time and again to ensure that the baskets were full every morning, but nothing changed. Pointing out the problem wasn't the issue; it was that the owner wasn't involving his manager in the vision. As it turned out, the baskets represented "bounty" to the owner. When they were half full, it felt "not bountiful" to him, the antithesis of the vision. When he shared the vision around the baskets and explained that they needed to be filled each morning, it made an impression on the manager; he started to see the importance of the baskets as he hadn't been able to before. The baskets were then filled every morning; the manager felt good about contributing to the vision of the owner, and the owner was pleased with his manager.

Leadership is not easy. So you must help develop this skill in our managers. For example, I worked with a corporate client who retained me to mentor the general manager as he wasn't "seeing" what the company leaders wanted him to see. The place was not being kept clean, and the cleaners were used to delivering a half-clean operation, and this manager never said anything. In working with this manager I had a two-pronged approach: I showed him what was in need of attention, and then we wrote out the expectations as a checklist.

In the walk-through I pointed out various aspects of the operation that were dingy and dusty. The floor to ceiling windows were only being washed halfway up and the top half was cloudy. The footrest at the bar was scuffed and was covered in dirty marks. The palm trees were dusty and had cobwebs. But showing these areas was not enough; together we created a checklist so that when the manager addressed the cleaning crew, he could be effective and succinct. The list was divided into "daily," "weekly," and "monthly" cleaning duties. The bar was a daily duty whereas the windows were a weekly duty. By having the manager write out the list, he could remember what was essential, and the list also set the expectation for cleanliness in the operation. By facing the cleaning crew and setting the standard with the crew, he was able to demonstrate his authority with this underperforming team. His attention to detail got crew members' attention, and they started showing improvement. And at any time when the standard was not met, the manager was empowered to talk about the standard, reinforce it, and ask for improvement. The place was cleaned, and the manager got results; this built his confidence in his role as someone in charge. And by upholding the standard, he built credibility and earned more respect from his team.

Being a manager is about building respect in your team. Respect is earned and your actions help you earn it, bit by bit. Employees want managers to set and hold them to the expectation. They want managers to notice when they uphold it and when they need some support. They also observe when other team members are not doing their job, and this is when the team will really need a manager to stand up for the standard: by ensuring that everyone is participating and contributing. Those who are not doing so must be spoken to, their behavior addressed, and then modified. Anything less reduces the manager's credibility.

Touching Your Guests

There is a convention in the restaurant businesses called "touching tables." It is a term that means checking in with the guests as they are seated at their tables. It is a manager's duty to check in with guests to say hello and gain feedback on the experience they are having. As a manager, my job was to check in with as many guests as possible whether it was welcoming them and taking them to their table, serving their food, or stopping by to ask how they were enjoying their experience. No matter how busy I was, this was always job #1 and our goal was always to "touch" as many tables and guests as possible.

"Touching," as defined by *New Oxford American Dictionary*, is pertinent to the job of manager: "arousing strong feelings of sympathy, appreciation, or gratitude." By taking time to address and engage with your guests, you will possibly inspire in them positive feelings about your business; when "appreciation" and "gratitude" are achieved, then you have done your job. Every manager should take time to engage with clients at many different times during their experience. It is an extension of the "I notice = I care" equation: when you notice your guests, they will feel cared for. People love to get picked out by the person in charge. It makes them feel special and like they matter to the business.

In a famous experiment conducted by the psychologist and social researcher Norbert Schwartz, researchers placed a dime on the top of a copy machine so that some people found a dime and others did not. After the experiment the participants were interviewed about their lives and those that found the dime "were more happy and more satisfied and wanted to change their lives less than those who didn't find a dime," Schwartz said in an article about the experiment in the *Baltimore Sun*.[1] The researchers conducted a second study in which they asked people leaving a grocery store to report on their satisfaction with their TV at home. Some of the people had received a free sample of cake just prior to being interviewed, and those who were given cake reported greater satisfaction with their TV.

It isn't about the reward, explains Schwartz. "It's that something positive happened to you."[2] This is because we give importance to our current mood, which is affected by finding a dime or receiving a free sample. This positivity colors our feelings about our current mood and serves to lighten up our current point of view on our lives. This is key to your impact as a manager. When you can give your attention to a guest in a nice little way (by noticing their situation), you can affect their mood and thoughts about their experience with the business. For example, when the manager can offer his card or a sample of merchandise or even a friendly hello, this can go a long way with guests as it helps create a positive impression of the present time, the time spent in your business.

"Touching your guests" is also about satisfaction. This is the moment where you can check in on your guests and find out if they are satisfied with their experience. When they are satisfied, you can create a bond with them on that basis. If they are satisfied you might say: "I'm so glad to hear that, thank you so much for telling me!" Or if they are not satisfied, you can help to do something about it: "I'm sorry you couldn't find that item on the shelf. Let me ring our stocker and see if there might be one in the back." Remember, service is active and intentional so when unintended events (you're out of stock) happen, you can offer an intentional solution. Taking a moment to interact with your guests allows that moment to happen.

In their study entitled "The Effect of Product Variety and Inventory Levels on Misplaced Products at Retail Stores," researchers Zynep Ton and Ananth Raman from Harvard studied 333 stores of a large retailer. They found that high numbers of misplaced products at a store had a massive effect on total sales. Customers would look for their product in the appropriate section of the store only to find it was "out of stock" on the shelf, but in fact it was stocked fully in a seemingly unrelated area (an endcap or promotional area). The researchers named the phenomenon a "phantom stockout," which costs the retail industry many millions of dollars in lost sales a year. The study authors report that at one bookseller, Borders Books, one out of six customers who approached a salesperson for help couldn't find a wanted item "not because the title was out-of-stock but rather because it was misplaced in a backroom, in other storage areas, or in the wrong aisle or location."[3] This is where the manager can be of great help to his guests. Being on the sales floor, helping the staff, and answering customer questions are all key to helping to ensure customer satisfaction and maintain healthy sales.

Service and sales are linked; you cannot have one without the other. And this is what makes the role of manager so important. As the "master of the house," you are able to increase sales, guest by guest. In my role as maître d', my job was to maximize sales by filling seats. In a restaurant the table is where the products are offered and purchased, and this is where managers have an impact as well. For example, being on the sales floor is important because then you are available to the staff and guests to answer questions and retrieve merchandise. As manager, you may have more flexibility to take time with a guest who requires more "hand-holding" than other customers. While your staff is attending to the guests for whom time is of the essence, you as manager can work with guests who need more information about a product, need a demonstration or explanation of differences between two similar items. Or you can just act as a friendly listener to those who want this special attention.

Supervisors often hold a dual role: contributing to the work at hand while also overseeing it. This can be great for the team as one team member is tasked with handling guest complaints, overseeing the shift, and maintaining quality while also contributing to dealing with the entire workload. Some operations like to keep their supervisors "under the radar" by having them wear the same uniform as other staff or only a slight variation of it. This means this supervisor is not always visible to the guests seeking a manager's touch. What this means is that this supervisor must be active in presenting his or her role to guests by being proactive, outgoing, and demonstrating managerial poise. For example, I was hired to coach a group of supervisors at a small business. I held a training session followed by an open forum where participants could ask questions, share best practices, and learn new leadership techniques.

The group shared a fear of having a customer ask "to see the manager." This was a dreaded situation because participants felt that if they were working alongside the other workers, when they announced their position, "I'm the supervisor, how may I help you?" it would be disregarded. There was one woman in the group who shared that she actually enjoyed this moment, as she was able to add value to her initial role by also being in charge. This was a great insight, and what we came up with was an image of the supervisors having a "Superman moment." They are working in Clark Kent mode alongside the others, but when someone needs special help or assistance, they are able to verbally change into "Superman" mode. Rather than shrinking away from the moment, they could see it as an opportunity: "I'm in charge, I'm right here, and I can help you immediately!" This distinction offered these supervisors a new perspective and helped them proudly interact with their guests in the moment of need. This empowerment helped the supervisors see that their presence in the business is important and that working alongside their teammates does not take away from their position.

One thing to add is that it is helpful for supervisors to have flexibility in their work role so that they can put their focus on the guest in need without slowing down the process or throughput of the other guests. This means that upper management must set up systems for the effectiveness of the supervisors helping customers. Chipotle demonstrates this often; supervisors float between the dining area, kitchen area, production line, and cashier and involve themselves wherever they are most needed. They are not essential to one particular position but are helpful as an "extra hand" where the need is greatest at the moment.

Spreading the Love

While "touching the guest" is a key part of being a manger and delivering a memorable customer service experience, it is also important for the manager to create a positive experience for the staff. A study entitled "What's Love Got To Do With It?" conducted by Sigal G. Barsade and Olivia A. O'Neill, researchers at Wharton Business School, proved that workplaces that uphold a more loving and affectionate culture for their staff experience lower turnover and improved job satisfaction. The researchers talk about the power of "companionate love," which is defined as "feelings of affection, compassion, caring, and tenderness for others" and is often found among coworkers at work. Companionate love has an importance in the workplace as it focuses on others. "Unlike 'self-focused' positive emotions (such as pride or joy), which center on independence and self-orientation," they write, "companionate love is an 'other-focused' emotion, promoting interdependence and sensitivity toward other people."[4] It is another "social emotion," and, like gratitude, it promotes and relies on the good feelings of the people around us.

This is the love you want to promote in your teams, especially in teams delivering customer service. The study found that organizations that foster more companionate love (hugs and kisses for greetings, care and concern for others' well-being) have lower turnover and higher levels of satisfaction than workplaces where the focus is on cognitive success (values that include results-oriented outcomes). In an article published in the *Harvard Business Review* under the title "Employees Who Feel Love Perform Better," the authors of the study write, "People who worked in a culture where they felt free to express affection, tenderness, caring, and compassion for one another were more satisfied with their jobs, committed to the organization, and accountable for their performance."[5]

This takes me back to the top. The social kissing at Balthazar had a great effect, not only on the numerous guests but on the entire staff as well. We all showed affection for one another across various lines in the operation: service staff and kitchen staff, servers and bussers, restaurant staff and bakery staff. This communal affection grew out of—and helped perpetuate—a culture of companionate love, a culture that creates a bond among the staff members that is deep and meaningful and that also includes the guests.

Managers can help build this culture and contribute to it. The warmth of an authentic greeting, a question about a loved one's health, or support for a team member who is going through a divorce—these are examples of what can help keep team members tethered to your business and able to deliver a consistently positive experience for your guests. Remember, managers lead the way by demonstrating the culture to their teams and guests. Participating in the culture is essential as it includes you as manager in the culture and helps you share it with your teams. Building core values based on the company culture is essential to living that culture every day. As a manager, you can do so much when you are able to uphold the company values in the work that you do.

I always like to use the core values as a basis on which to hire new personnel. Use the core values as a starting point for a question to better understand whether the applicant would be a good fit for your business. Rather than asking a potential employee to tell you about his or her last position, use the core value of integrity to pose a clearer question. "Give me an example of how you stood up for your business or coworker at your last job." Candidates who can answer this authentically are telling you they have already learned the lesson and already uphold the values of your business. Our goal in hiring is to ensure our staff members will embody our core values and represent the brand, culture, and personality of our business. When someone already shares the same values, there are fewer hurdles to cross; staff member showing affinity for the core values of your business "speak the same language" as you do.

The loving relationship between your staff and guests is real. Your guests will love your staff, and your staff will love your guests—if you allow them to. Encouraging a culture of love and mutual respect is a two-way street of satisfaction, and you as manager are the one who needs to make sure there is always a green light. You must encourage the positive interaction between your staff members and guests; staff members are the ambassadors of your brand and will represent you however you want. This means you must be clear and consistent yourself. You must recognize and call out bad behavior, but you must also reward and acknowledge good behavior. Your team members need this, and when your team members feel good, your guests are more likely to feel good also.

The authors of the "What's Love Got To Do With It" study offer three points of advice for mangers: First, expand your culture to include emotional elements, be it love, joy, or group pride. Second, leaders must pay attention to their own moods and emotions as leaders truly create the "cultural blueprint"[6] for the business. Third, leaders should assess company procedures for how compassionate and caring they are and make changes that offer flexibility for employees enduring difficult life events (death in the family, divorce). The goal here is to further compassion in the workplace. Finally, the study authors share this piece of wisdom about colleagues sharing and managers upholding the culture of love in the workplace: let employees show affection and support toward one another at work and see them flourish and grow with your company. Creating an experience for your staff members is just as important as creating an experience for your guests; your positive actions and the culture you create will make a big impact on the people you employ and the people you serve.

Tips and Takeaways

- **Start with You**. Your mood dictates the culture and service of your company. Set yourself up for success and check in with your needs during your day. Check your energy levels and make sure you are able to perform at 100 percent. Make sure you are hydrated and well-fed; this job is very active, and you must be energetic and aware as you work with your team and with your guests. Turn this attention on your staff as well; make sure your team members are taking breaks and take time to rest and recover and restore themselves between shifts. Everyone must come to work energized and ready to be there for the guests.

- **Thank YOU!** Businesses love long-time employees and must reward longevity. Some businesses offer a day of vacation on the anniversary of their first day of work. Offering a celebratory one-day bonus to your team is a nice way to say "thank you" to them, and when you announce various anniversaries and the years of service, it can serve to be inspirational to the newbies as well. In some operations I have seen many an employee come to work on his or her anniversary to celebrate with teammates and management rather than be away from the workplace. This is a nice sign of continued devotion to the brand and the managers that uphold it.

- **Innovate the Service Experience.** Ask your management team members to consider ways to impact the staff experience and the guest experience. Ask them to think of promotions for customers or opportunities for growing sales for the team. Both can be a vehicle for educating, informing, and sharing with both customers and staff members while building sales and sales opportunities for staff members.

- **Feedback, Feedback, Feedback.** This is crucial for the success of your business, as we have discussed throughout the book. Feedback is essential for your growth as a manager as well. Conduct 360 feedback for your management staff members; invite feedback from their colleagues, from those they manage, and from those who manage them. Leave out the comments that are glowing or scathing and focus on the commonalities that can help a person grow his or her skills. Hearing that you are respected for your efficiency, but your team feels that you are too hard on yourself is an interesting perspective. One that people can work to adjust and change. Institute a "feed forward" method with your teams; this means the leader gives feedback to the team members, and the members give feedback to the leader as well. This can help level the playing field and allows everyone room for growth and collaboration in building skills and removing blockages. Feedback can be a great part of the culture; make sure it is given with compassion and empathy and that it is always helpful not hurtful.

Notes

1 Hello: The First Important Thing

1. "Zappos Family Core Values," http://www.zappos.com/d/about-zappos-culture (accessed August 25, 2015).

3 The Power of Chairs, Doors, and Stairs

1. Ryan Sutton, "$1Billion Plaza Hotel Means $100 Tea, $26 Pancakes: Food Buzz," http://www.bloomberg.com/apps/news?sid=a.u61WdKFUwM&pid=newsarchive (accessed on March 18, 2008).
2. L. Williams and J. Ackerman, (December 15, 2011), "Please Touch the Merchandise," https://hbr.org/2011/12/please-touch-the-merchandise/ (accessed on August 25, 2015).
3. J. M. Ackerman, C. C. Nocera, and J. A. Bargh, (2010). "Incidental Haptic Sensations Influence Social Judgments and Decisions." *Science* 328 (5986), 1712–15; doi:10.1126/science.1189993.
4. L. E. Williams and J. A. Bargh, (2008). "Experiencing Physical Warmth Promotes Interpersonal Warmth." *Science* 322 (5901), 606–7; doi:10.1126/science.1162548.
5. Ibid.
6. Tim Hindle, (October 14, 2009). "The Halo Effect." *The Economist*, http://www.economist.com/node/14299211.

4 Please Hold

1. David Maister, (1985). "The Psychology of Waiting Lines," in John A. Czepiel, Michael R. Solomon, and Carol Suprenant (eds.), *The Service Encounter* (New York: D. C. Heath).

5 Say What?

1. Predictive Group, (2015) "Predictive Index Customer Service Rep (CSR) Study," http://www.predictivegroup.com/predictive-index-performance-snapshots/predictive-index-performance-snapshots-1, (accessed on May 28, 2015).

2. J. C. Richards, J. Platt, and H. Platt, (1997). *Longman Dictionary of Language Teaching and Applied Linguistics* (New York: Longman), 144.

3. F. Heylighen and J. M. Dewaele, (1999). "Formality of Language: Definition, Measurement and Behavioral Determinants," Internal Report, Center "Leo Apostel," Free University of Brussels.

6 There Is No Such Thing as Medium Rare

1. Julia Layton, "How Fear Works," September 13, 2005. HowStuffWorks.com. <http://science.howstuffworks.com/life/inside-the-mind/emotions/fear.htm>, (accessed on May 28, 2015).

2. K. Jimura, M. S. Chushak, and T. S. Braver, (2013) "Impulsivity and Self-Control during Intertemporal Decision Making Linked to the Neural Dynamics of Reward Value Representation," *The Journal of Neuroscience* 33 (1): 344–57; doi: 10.1523/JNEUROSCI.0919–12.2013.

7 A Little Decency

1. Steve Harrison, (2007). *The Manager's Book of Decencies: How Small Gestures Build Great Companies* (New York: McGraw-Hill), 10.

8 From Dust to Mistrust

1. Rick Blizzard, (September 10, 2002). "Do Patients Equate Cleanliness with Quality?" http://www.gallup.com/poll/6784/patients-equate-cleanliness-quality.aspx (accessed on May 28, 2015).

9 What Brings Regulars Back

1. Thanx, "6 Critical Stats for Customer Loyalty," http://info.thanx.com/6-critical-stats-for-customer-loyalty (accessed on May 22, 2015).

2. Robert Cialdini, (1984). *Influence: The Psychology of Persuasion* (New York: William Morrow), 60.

3. Ibid.

4. Ibid., 57.

10 When Things Go Wrong

1. Jake Poore, (January 19, 2010). "Service Recovery," http://www.jakepoore.com/2010/01/19/service-recovery/ (accessed on May 28, 2015).

2. "Good Service Is Good Business: American Consumers Willing to Spend More with Companies That Get Service Right, According to American Express Survey," May 3, 2011, http://about.americanexpress.com/news/pr/2011/csbar.aspx (accessed on May 22, 2015).

3. 2014 "Convergys US Customer Scorecard Research. Key Findings on Customer Loyalty and Satisfaction," http://www.convergys.com/pdf/research /POV014-2014-Scorecard-Research.pdf?TRID=1 (accessed on August 29, 2015).

4. M. Waldman and A. Newberg, MD, "The Most Dangerous Word in the World," August 1, 2012, https://www.psychologytoday.com/blog/words-can -change-your-brain/201208/the-most-dangerous-word-in-the-world (accessed on August 29, 2015).

11   The Old-Fashioned Touch

1. S. Dolcos, K. Sung, J. J. Argo, S. Flor-Henry, and F. Dolcos, (December 2012). "The Power of a Handshake: Neural Correlates of Evaluative Judgments in Observed Social Interactions," *Journal of Cognitive Neuroscience* 24 (12): 2292–305.

2. Steve McGaughey, (October 19, 2012). "Science Reveals the Power of a Handshake." *Beckman Institute*, Beckman.illinois.edu (accessed on May 13, 2015).

3. W. F. Chaplin, J. B. Phillips, J. D. Brown, N. R. Clanton, and J. L. Stein, (2000). "Handshaking, Gender, Personality and First Impression," *Journal of Personality and Social Psychology* 79: 110–17.

4. Bethela, *The Etsy Blog*, (June 12, 2008), https://blog.etsy.com/en/2008/service -tips-for-sellers-packaging-and-shipping/.

5. John Coleman, (April 5, 2013). "Handwritten Notes are a Rare Commodity: They're also More Important Than Ever." *Harvard Business Review*, HBR. org.

6. Guy Winch, (November 21, 2013). "The Five Ingredients of an Effective Apology," *Psychology Today* (accessed on May 13, 2015).

12   Don't Scratch That Itch

1. Michelle R. Van Dellen and Rick H. Hoyle, (2010). "Regulatory Accessibility and Social Influences on State Self-Control," *Personality and Social Psychology Bulletin*, 36: 251–63.

2. Sylvia Ann Hewlett, (2014). *Executive Presence: The Missing Link Between Merit and Success* (New York: Harper Business), 5.

3. Robert Bacal, (2011). *If It Wasn't for the Customers I'd Really Like this Job: Stop Angry, Hostile Customers COLD While Remaining Professional, Stress-Free, Efficient, and Cool as a Cucumber* (Create Space Independent Publishing Platform), 44.

4. Ibid., 47.

5. Ibid., 38.

6. Robert Bacal, (2010). *Defusing Hostile Customers Workbook: A Self-Instructional Workbook for Public Sector Employees,* 3rd ed. (New York: McGraw-Hill), 31.

14 Every Time I Say Good-Bye

1. Robert Emmons, (November 16, 2010). "Why Gratitude Is Good," *Greater Good*, http://greatergood.berkeley.edu (accessed on May 13, 2015).
2. Ibid.
3. William Bridges, (2004). *Transitions: Making Sense of Life's Changes, Strategies for Coping with the Difficult, Painful, and Confusing Times in Your Life*, 2nd ed. (New York: Da Capo Press), 107.

15 The Manager of Small Things

1. Susan Ager, (August 22, 1999). "A Dime Can Make a Difference," *The Baltimore Sun*, http://articles.baltimoresun.com/1999-08-22.
2. Ibid.
3. Z. Ton and A. Rahman, (June 2004). "The Effect of Product Variety and Inventory Levels on Misplace Products at Retail Stores: A longitudinal Study," Stern.NYU.edu, http://pages.stern.nyu.edu/~gjanakir/Ton_and_Raman6-10 -04.pdf.
4. S. Barsade and O. A. O'Neill, (2014). "What's Love Got to Do with It? A Longitudinal Study of Companionate Love and Employee and Client Outcomes in a Long-Term Care Setting." *Administrative Science Quarterly*, http://mgmt .wharton.upenn.edu.
5. S. Barsade and O. A. O'Neill, (January 13, 2014). "Employees Who Feel Love Perform Better." *Harvard Business Review*, hbr.org.
6. Ibid.

Index